Planned and Unplanned Parenthood, 1850 - 1870

Originally published in 1876 as
Dr. Youman's Illustrated Marriage Guide and Confidential Adviser
by J. Fletcher & Co.

Metheglin Press
Phoenix, Arizona

Planned and Unplanned Parenthood,
1850 - 1870

is a complete transcription of

*Dr. Youman's Illustrated Marriage Guide
and Confidential Medical Adviser*

Copyright 1876 by J. Fletcher & Co.

Modern introduction, notes, index, and glossary
by Katie F. Hamilton
New Material Copyright 2001 Katie F. Hamilton

ISBN 1-889023-11-6

http://MetheglinPress.com

Printed by PrintPartner,
Phoenix, Arizona

TABLE OF CONTENTS

Publisher's Note.

. The source of this edition deserves special mention. Sized 4.5" x 6.25" x 0.5", the original book has 265 yellowed pages of tiny print, 9 lines per inch. Pages are hand-stitched between two thin pieces of leather. The flesh-side is used for the book's outside, the red Moroccan leather surface is on the inside; this is probably salvaged leather. The title is handwritten on paper and glued to the front cover.

Text--except for ten pages of advertisements--was probably copied from an earlier publication, clearly without input from Dr. Youman. Misspelled homonyms in lieu of medical terms support that conclusion.

Illustrations--some are mere blobs--did not age as well as the text. The author named several scientists responsible for drawings of specimen. He did not, however, tells us how he obtained these drawing.

Finally, drilling ten holes in a half-inch stack of paper and sewing the pages with cotton cord may have served a dual purpose: 1, it was cheaper than proper binding. 2, parents who bought this book for a daughter about to be married, could cut the cord, remove the gruesome descriptions of infections and VD, and re-sew the pages. Sadly confused by the irrelevant plant and animal data, the daughter might not notice the missing pages. Had she seen the complete text, she might have broken off the engagement and opted for the single life.

Introduction

The Victorian Age, 1837 to 1901, put an indelible stamp on Great Britain and the United States. Sharing more than a common language, both countries embraced gains and losses of the industrial revolution, of nationalist expansion, and of ever faster travel and communications. Darwin's theories suggested that mankind might attain perfection through deliberate mate-selection, and scientists delved ever deeper into the secrets of nature. In that impatient age, enthusiasm greeted new discoveries; they became inventions, processes, or cures. Scientists and inventors foresaw no limit to progress.

Yet, on hearing "Victorian," we envision carpets, drapery, paintings, and pillows covering every surface. In contrast to that decorative excess, we recall rigidly conventional lives, idle Sundays as proof of religion observed, and men free to do as they pleased; after all, wives and children belonged to husbands or fathers like personal property.

We also recall accounts of great poverty, high infant mortality, and debilitating diseases without cure.

No wonder that the gulf between ideas and reality, between the empowered and the powerless, between the thriving and the barely surviving gave rise to Marxism, Anarchism and labor unrest.

Many physicians, teachers and preachers tried to help the barely literate survive and prosper through religious tracts and self-help books. Affordable for people who could not engage a specialist, Dr. Youman's Illustrated Marriage Guide of 1876 is typical of such books.

Dr. Youman stresses the need for accurate information about sexual reproduction. His examples, however, cover the reproductive mechanics of flowers, insects, and vertebrates. Youman enumerates the similarity of embryonic development in various species and among all mammalians. The chapter immediately following this biology lesson covers health and treatment of newborn babies.

City-bred girls might read these lectures and never discern how human semen reached the human ovum. Youman's chapters for young men and young women urge great caution when selecting a mate, the need for chastity before and during marriage, and the dreadful results of masturbation. He stresses that the sole purpose of marriage is procreation and declares that intercourse during pregnancy or lactation is injurious to mother and baby.

Dr. Youman compares human mate selection for optimum offspring to the best practices of horse and cattle breeders. His detailed instructions cover desirable and undesirable features of a potential spouse.

Totally ineffective treatments of venereal diseases justify Youman's call for lifelong chastity. The marriage guide's appendix, Ready Remedies for Common Complaints, shows available cures before the dawn of new discoveries--their dates are shown below.

Medical Timeline:

1852 to 1877 L. Pasteur proves that micro-organisms cause fermentation.

1875 J. Lister uses disinfectants during surgery.

1877 R. Koch stains bacteria in diseased tissue and proves that every disease has a specific cause.

1879 A. L. S. Neisser identifies cause of gonorrhea.

1884 K. S. Crede uses silver nitrate drops to prevent blindness of newborns whose mothers had gonorrhea.

1906 Schaudium & Hoffmann identify the bacterium that causes syphlilis.

1906 A. Wasserman develops a test for syphilis.

1910 P. Ehrlich develops arsenic chemotherapy, the first effective cure for syphilis.

CHAPTER I.

[Descriptions replace drawings no longer recognizable. Figures marked >> follow page 202.]

In the following treatise we purpose treating in a plain, common sense manner, that all may understand, the important problems relating to sexual physiology.

The function of reproduction is the most important in the animal economy because the continuance of the race depends upon it. From the simplest vegetable to the highest form of animal life, a mysterious power is continually in operation--a power which did it cease to exist all plants and animals would perish from the earth. It is this wonderful and mysterious power of reproduction through its various forms and processes which we purpose to examine and deduct lessons for our edification and guidance.

In the vegetable kingdom, where this phenomenon may be most conveniently examined, there are several modes of reproduction; even the same plant may have two or three distinct methods of propagating its kind. Let us look at our lovely friend of the earliest spring-time, the crocus. Each bulb sends up its flower, and each flower produces germs and pollen. The germ is formed in the ovary or female organ of the flower; the pollen is formed upon the anther, the top of the stamen or male organ. The pollen, a cell containing the masculine element, fertilizes the germ-cell, or feminine element; in some way, incomprehensible to us, the union of the two elements results in the formation of the living germ, which under favorable circumstances, develops into the perfect plant, which in turn produces new flowers and seeds.

The flower of every plant, and its seed or fruit, is the consummation of its life. On flowers nature has lavished all her ingenuity of construction and adaptation, beauty, perfume, and sweetness. In most plants the masculine and feminine elements are in the same flower, stamens and pistils growing almost in contact. In upright flowers the stamens are longest so that the

1

pollen can fall upon the pistil; in drooping flowers it is the reverse. The snow-drop at first holds up its pure petals to the sun, but when the period comes for the masculine and feminine elements to form the living germs of new beings, it modestly hangs down its head, and it is this change which makes the union possible.

"One analogy," says Flint, "of the world of animal life is still preserved, and the male-flowers as the stronger and bolder sex, are drawn by the impulses of Nature to pay court to the feebler and more delicate female. The male stamina, with their gayly painted hats, bow around the female pistil as beaux around their belle. Each in turn is permitted to come in contact with the fair, and as the contact takes place, the golden pollen is shaken upon the pistil, and the stamen retires to give place to the next that offers the same hommage. The mystery of fructification is accomplished, and the flower-cup is fecundated.

"There are stamina which can not reach half the height of their beloved pistils. Nature then varies the arrangement, so as not to be defeated in her object. The Lilliputions strive in vain to reach their Brobdignag Venus. As they can not come to her she condescendingly comes down to them. It is in this way that the crown imperial and harebell hang upon their stems, which position, so graceful in the flower, is a foresight of Nature. The pollen of the stamens comes in contact with the stigma of the pistil by falling upon it. As soon as the mystery is accomplished and the flower-cup fecundated, the stalk which sustains the flower turns it up to the sky. Its bower of love was concealed, but it shows the cradle of its children.

"Wherever you see flowers gently inclining their bells toward the turf, you may infer that the stamens within are shorter than the pistil. There are plants, the habits of whose loves are still more amusing. They are the wedded dames who in compassion to their little husbands, slightly bend their elastic persons, contemplate them for a moment, and afterward erect themselves, still bearing marks of their yielding weakness. Such are the loves of the passion-flower and the willow-herb."

Many flowers are provided with organs which secrete honey; this honey is stored in deep vases, very deep sometimes, as the Columbine Bees and other insects, and even some birds, as the humming bird, attracted by the honey, and seeking it in its deep cells, unconsciously aid in the process of generation. The pollen adheres to their bodies or wings, and is brought in contact with the stigma of the same flower, or others of the same species, to which they are made to adhere by a viscid secretion. All flowers do not contain both male and female organs of generation. They may be on different parts of the same plant, as in the maize, or corn, where the pollen is produced on the very top of the tall stalk, sometimes twenty feet high, while the long silky pistils grow from the cob which holds the germs in rows about the middle of the stalk. Sometimes the male and female flowers are on different trees or plants, and their propagation is entirely dependent upon insects or favoring breezes.

When the pollen cell, containing the fecundating element falls upon the stigma of a flower, adhering to its viscid secretion, a very beautiful vital process commences. The inner membrane of the pollen extends itself into a tube which penetrates into the style, which is sometimes two or three inches in length, until it reaches the germ in the ovary, where it penetrates the germ, or meets a corresponding tube thrown out by it. The two elements unite, the germ is fertilised and grows into a seed, the egg of the plant, in which is formed, and from which is developed the new plant which is to continue the species. The living germ of the plant is very small, quite microsopic in its dimension. The seeds of plants contain albuminous and oily matter, destined to be the first food of the young plant, and which also, in such seeds as those of wheat, barley, rice, peas, beans, &c., furnish important stores of food for men and animals.

If we examine such seeds, we shall find the real germ to be a mere speck, a microsopic cell, which must, however, contain potentially the future plant or tree, and all it is capable of producing; it must contain form, character, color, odor, and the directive or formative principle which governs its whole life and development. And this character of the plant, observe, resides in the two elements, male and female, which join to produce it, for by bringing together these elements, gardeners are able to produce all kinds of crosses, hybrids, and varieties.

Fig. 1, Section of Pistil >>

The reproduction or continuation of the species of plants by this process is called true generation; but this is not the only mode by which vegetable life is continued or extended. The bulb of our crocus which sends up a stalk, leaves, and flowers also throws out from its side the fibres which form new bulbs, which the following season separate from the parent bulb, and themselves produce bulbs and flowers.

Take now a tuberous plant--the potato. It has its pretty flowers, and produces balls full of seeds which will produce new plants, and varieties; but at the same time there grow out from the roots great tubers, and on these are buds which will grow into perfect plants, producing in turn seeds and tubers. The strawberry has also a double method of propagation. It produces flowers and seeds, but it also throws out long vines, which at intervals send down roots on which grow plants, and so on until a whole field is covered with them.

We imitate these processes of nature in multiplying plants and trees--of one making many. Ladies cut slips of geraniums, roses and other plants, placing them in pots of moist sand or earth where the covered buds send out roots, and those exposed to the light expand into leaves. The Chinese multiply fruit trees by molding a ball of earth upon a twig, keeping it moist, and making a section in the bark below it. When roots have penetrated the earth they cut it off and plant it. Each bud of a tree has its distinct life, and in most cases can be transferred to another tree of an allied species and made to grow, producing, however, its own peculiar flowers and fruit. Each bud is a germ; the seed germs are similar, but differ at least in this, that they sometimes produce as in potatoes and apples, new varieties.

A bud or graft gives us the same fruit as its parent tree. A tree which grows from an apple seed may produce very different fruit. For this reason, when fruit trees are grown from seeds, gardeners bud or graft them; that is transfer to them buds or twigs from trees producing a favorite variety, and let the transferred buds grow to form the future trees.

4

Low forms of vegetation, as the various kinds of fungi and ferns are produced from spores, which are germs or rudimental buds rather than seeds. They are very small, produced by myriads, as in the puff ball, and are so light as to be blown about by the winds, and almost fill the atmosphere. Wherever air can penetrate, it carries with it the germs of vegetation as well as those of the lower forms of animal life.

But it is in our lovely and odorous flowers that we have the highest types of the generation of vegetable life; and the favorite science of Botany largely consists of the study of the organs and processes of vegetable reproduction, or what the Elder Darwin in his curious poem calls the Loves of the Plants, which present us with the most delightful analogies to the higher processes of reproduction in animals and our own species. Botany is therefore a charming introduction to all other branches of natural history, and especially to that branch of human physiology which we are now considering.

CHAPTER II
Animal Reproduction -- The Origin of Life

Reproduction in animals is curiously analogous to the same process in the vegetable kingdom. There are the same varieties in the modes of mutiplication and generation. The process of generation in some of the lower animal organizations is exactly like the throwing out of new bulbs in plants. The polyps throw out buds which in a little while grow mouths, fringed with cilla or tentacles, while they are still holding by stalks, and drawing part of their nourishment from their parents. When enough matured to get their own living they drop off, swim away, and shift for themselves. This is germination.

Fission is a common mode of propagation or multiplication among the infusoria. An animalcule is seen to contract in a ring around its centre; the fissure deepens, and it divides into two distinct beings, which also divide, and so on--multiplying with surprising rapidity. It has been estimated that one of these animalcules could produce by these successive divisions in eight weeks a progeny of two hundred and sixty-eight millions. This reproductive power is, however, almost rivalled by some fishes and insects. The carp lays seven hundred thousand eggs in a season, and lives two hundred years. The possible progeny of a pair of these fishes is almost beyond computation. The cod is said to produce from four to nine millions of eggs. The female termite lays sixty thousand eggs a day for a considerable period.

Some of the lower animals may be multiplied artificially like vegetables. Thus, if some species of the polyps are cut in pieces, each piece produces the missing parts, so as to become a perfect animal, as cuttings of a geranium produce geraniums.

But perhaps the most curious mode of multiplication takes place in some sea-worms. They divide into sections by constricting rings, and each section forms for itself head, eyes, &c., at one extremity, and tail at the other, while yet the sections are united; but when all is ready each section sets up its own independent life, and then produces in its body germs of similar worms, by the more usual process--just as some vegetables propagate by seeds, as well as by bulbs or tubers.

These modes of multiplication--fission, germination, &c., such as I have described are, however, not the rule in nature, but the exception, or variation--a ruder method of the extension of life, which is confined to the lower forms of animal existence.

As vegetables are generally produced from seeds, animals are generally produced from eggs. It has long been a disputed question with the learned, as to whether life can be produced, under certain circumstances from inanimate substances, independent of egg or seed, without parental source. Numerous experiments have been tried to solve this problem, and some have seemed to determine the question affirmatively, but more searching investigation has detected the fallacy of the experiments, and at present the majority of Physiologists disbelieve the doctrine of spontaneous generation.

There is no good reason, so far as we now know, to believe that there is any spontaneous generation of vegetables or animals--that is, that any vegetable or animal ever of itself is formed from matter without a spore or germ which has been produced by a similar organization. At some time, and in some way, every kind of living form has its beginning; but no one has seen such beginnings. Creation is a mystery. Every living thing upon the earth has at some time, somewhere and somehow been created; but we do not know the when, the where, or the how.

Human science reveals to us something of the phenomena of nature--nothing of its causes or beginnings.

As in vegetables we find the beginning of new organizations in the formation by the generative organs of a plant, which are in most cases portions of its flower, of a germ cell in the ovary or female organ, and of a pollen cell by the anthor or male organ, which unite to form the living germ, which develops into the perfect plant--so in all the higher forms of animal life, in oysters, fishes, insects, birds, beasts and men, we have germs or eggs formed in the ovaries of the female, which at a certain stage of development are impregnated, or fecundated by union with a similar germ, produced in a somewhat similar organ of the male--the male and female elements uniting to produce the perfect being. The unfertilised, unimpregnated, or unfecundated ovum or egg quickly perishes. The one to which has been added the masculine element is from that moment endowed with life, and, with favoring conditions, developes with a wonderful rapidity.

Fishes produce a vast number of eggs, as may be seen in the hard roe of herring, which, when they have arrived at a certain stage, are spawned--that is, expelled from the body in places which the fish instinctively find for that purpose. Salmon come hundreds, perhaps thousands of miles, through the deep ocean to lay their eggs in the shallow fresh water streams in which they themselves were hatched. The male herring and salmon produce, in organs not unlike the ovaries, myriads of sperm cells, destined to fertilize the germ cells of the female. This is the soft roe--a brain-like substance, chiefly composed of these cells. The male fishes attend the females, and fill the water where their eggs are laid with what seems a milky fluid. The two elements come into contact, perhaps by mutual attraction, fecundation takes place, and, in due time, swarms of young fishes are the result.

With insects and birds, the process is a little varied. The eggs are formed, as with the fishes, in the ovaries of the females, but at a certain stage they are fecundated before leaving the body, by the male element being conveyed to them by a proceess similar to that which takes place in flowers. The seminal fluid of the male, corresponding to the pollen of the plant, is conveyed to the germ in the ovary by means specially adapted to that purpose. After the egg has grown to its full size--in insects covered with a tough membrane, and in birds with a hard shell--it is placed in some proper nest, and hatched either by solar heat or the warmth of one or both of the parents. Animals so born are called oviparous--born from eggs. A few fishes, as the shark and skate, lay fecundated eggs like birds, with curiously formed horny shells and cable for mooring.

With the mammalia, the higher orders of animals, including the human species, there is still another process.

The egg or germ is formed in the ovary of the female. When fully formed, it bursts from its containing membranes, with a certain degree of excitement of the generative system, and passes through tubes provided for that purpose into a receptacle called uterus, or womb. If here met by the seminal fluid, or fertilizing masculine element, fecundation takes place, a perfect germ is produced, foetal life begins, and the animal is, so to speak, hatched in the womb of its mother, nourished by her blood, and grows until it is ready to come into the world and live its independent life. Animals so produced are called viviparous, or born alive.

The young of the kangaroo, and other marsupials, are born in a very immature condition, and carried in a kind of bag formed upon the abdomen of the mother, within which are the teats from which the little ones draw their nourishment.

The eggs of birds, from those of the humming-bird, like peas, to the great eggs of the ostrich, which will furnish a dinner for six men, contain not only the germ, which is very minute, but its supply of food--the materials from which its body bones, feathers, &c., are formed, during the process of incubation or hatching. The white of the egg, almost pure albumen, is not essential to it, but useful as food. The eggs of many animals are without it. The yolk, consisting of albumen and oil, contains the matter first taken into the organization. The germinal spot, a point of matter, is the real germ, and can only be seen under the microscope. The eggs of viviparous animals are of extreme minuteness. That of a dog is the 1/100 of an inch in diameter including yolk, germinal vesicle, and germinal spot. The human ovum is still smaller, about 1/140 of an inch in diameter; and in the circumference of that small diameter lies, what a world of character and power!--lies all that shall distinguish the highest example of human civilization and culture, from the lowest savage--poet, philosopher, hero, idiot, ruffian, lunatic--all the possibilites and potentialities of humanity.

CHAPTER III
The Organs of Generation

In the human race, as throughout the greater part of the animal kingdom, generation is accomplished by fecundation, or the effect of the vivifying fluid provided by one class of organs upon the germ contained in the seed or ovum formed by another class, in the opposite sex. This germ, when fecundated, is termed the embryo. The process consists of impregnation in the male, conception in the female.

> Fig. 2, "The Nervous System," a silhouette of the human form, labeled: 1, the cerebrum; 2, cerebellum; 3, spinal chord; 4, nerves of the face; 5, the bracial plexus or union of nerves; 6, 7, 8, 9, nerves of the arm; 10, those that pass under the ribs; 11, lumbar plexus; 12, sacral plexus; 13, 14, 15, 16, nerves of lower limbs.

The organs of generation in the male are:

1. The testes and their envelopes, namely, the scrotum or cutaneous envelope: the dartos, which corrugates or ridges the scrotum; and the fibrous or vaginal tunics; we must also here include the epidermis, above the testes; the vas deferens, or excretory duct, and the spermatic chord.

2. *Vesiculæ seminales*, forming a canal situated beneath the bladder.

3. The prostate gland, surrounding the neck of the bladder and the commencement of the urethra.

4. Cowper's glands, a pair situated below the prostate.

5. The ejaculatory ducts.

6. The penis, which consists of the *corpus cavernosum*, the urethra, the *corpus spongiosum*, which terminates in the glans penis; then there are the vessels, nerves, and a cutaneous investment, which by its prolongation forms the prepuce.

The female organs are:

1. The *vulva* or *pudendum*, the external parts, comprehending the labia pudendi, the clitoris, situated at the middle and superior part of the pudendum; the *nymphæ* or *alæ minores*; the urethra, which terminates in the *meatus urinarius*, opening into the

vagina, which is occupied by the hymen, a semilunar fold or the *carunculæ myrtiformis*, its lacerated remains, and the entrance into the vagina, termed the *os externum*, so called to distinguish it from the internum, or orifice of--

2. The uterus, whose appendages are: the *ligamenta lata* (the broad ligaments), sometimes called *alæ vespertilionum*, and the round ligaments commencing immediately before and below the Fallopian tubes, which extend to the ovaria.

The Perinæum.--The space between the anus and the external parts of the generative organs, so called from being frequently moist. The operation of cutting for stone in males is usually performed here.

The Bladder is the receptacle for the urine, which it receives by drops from the ureters, the conduits from the kidneys. In shape, the bladder is somewhat like a pear; but it is much modified by the quantity of its contents, and the relative condition of the neighboring parts. For instance, when the bladder is full, its upper part may be distinguished as rising above the *Pubes*, or that portion of the lower part of the abdomen that is covered with hair. The bladder is composed of several coats. There is a peculiar membrane investing the important structures in the abdomen called the *peritoneum*. The fundis and back part of the bladder is covered by a portion of this peritonum, which serves in some measure to support the bladder in its position.

Fig. 3. Urinary Bladder. Silhouette labeled: 8 Left ureter. 9 Left portion of seminal vesicles. 11 lateral lobes of the prostate gland. 14 Urethra tied with cord.

The muscular coats of the bladder are very strong; they consist of fibres running in three diferent directions. An idea of their strength may be given, when it is stated that the bladder is capable of containing per force, two or three pints of urine, the whole of which can be ejected to the last drop.

The ureters open very obliquely into the bladder, for the twofold purpose of preventing a retrogression of the urine, and its too rapid descent into the bladder. The bladder, as the urine accumulates in it, becomes sensibly excited to contraction and hence the discharge.

The kidneys, which appear to form so insignificant an item in the human body, are among the most important structures in its economy. By some wonderful, yet inexplicable process, the waste fluid of the body, except that given off by perspiration and exhalation, passes through them. All we know of the matter is, that the blood in its circulation wends its way through especial arteries called the *Renal*, and comes out through the ureters in the form of urine, the rapidity of which process, in some instance is most astonishing. Diseases of the kidneys form a serious malady, and often jeopardize the life of man. The kidneys will be perceived to be situated in the upper part of the loins.

The kidneys are usually embedded in fat. The exterior coat of the kidney is very vascular, and the interior consists of tubes collected into conical points that open into the pelvis of the kidney.

Fig. 4, Section of a kidney. Silhouette without notation.

CHAPTER IV.
Germination, Fecundation and Impregnation

At a certain period in the life of a plant, in organs prepared for that important function, are formed the germs of new plants. The germ-producing organ, frond or flower, does its work and dies. The tree lives on, but each individual bud, producing flower and seed or fruit perishes. This is the law of vegetative generation. Such is also, to a great extent, the law of insect life.

Fig. 5, Renal Gland of Owl >>
Fig. 6, Back of Body >>
Fig. 7, Course of Circulation >>

The insect produces one crop of germs; they are fertilized by one conjunction of the sexes; the eggs are deposited, sometimes in immense numbers, where they can be hatched in safety, and where its proper food can be found for the new being in the earliest stage of its development; and then, as if the whole purpose of life had been accomplished, the male and female alike perish. In some cases the male insect sacrifices his life in the very act of fecundation.

In the higher orders of animals, fishes, reptiles, birds, and mammals, the production of germs goes on year after year in varying periods. The guinea pig begins to breed at two months old, and the higher the type, the later is the period of germ formation, until in man the period of puberty, or the beginning of the generative function, is at about fifteen years, varying from twelve to eighteen; but the natural powers are scarcely at their full strength and fitness until some years later.

The power of reproduction as to numbers seems to be in the inverse ratio as to development. The lowest forms of life multiply with amazing rapidity; some insects produce myriads, fishes spawn eggs by millions, hens lay an egg a day for months together, rabbits, cats, dogs breed every few months, and have at each birth a numerous progeny, while the higher orders of mammalia produce their young but once a year, and have but one, or, in rare cases, two at a birth. When the human germ has been slowly formed in the ovary, and perfected up to the period when it bursts forth in its first birth, fit for impregnation, it is nine months in arriving at the development which fits it for birth and independent existence. For twelve months more it draws its supply of nutriment from the mother, and two years may be considered the normal interval from birth to birth. It should never be less with a proper regard to the health of the mother, and the proper development of her children; and the practice of shortening this period by hiring wet nurses is a violation of nature, which is avenged on parents and their offspring. The mother is exhausted by too frequent child bearing, and children are deprived of the love, the magnetism, the life of the mother, which comes to them from her blood transformed into the most delicious food for them, and the nervous and spiritual food which no money can buy, and no one but the mother can give. The human germ cell, or egg, is formed from the blood in a gland-like organ, about an inch and a half long, oval shaped placed in the lower part of the abdomen, in the groin, and situated on each side of the uterus, or womb.

In each ovary, from the period of puberty, in a healthy female, there is a constant formation and growth of germs, or ova, which goes on for thirty or forty years. When the first perfect germs have ripened, one or more, they come to the surface of the ovary, burst from their sacs, sometimes with considerable force, attended by a nervous exitement, a congestion of the blood vessels of ovaries and womb, and, when impregnation does not take place, the freed germ passes into the mouth of the Fallopian tube, through which it passes into the uterus, from which it passes, with the menstrual evacuation, a secretion from the mucous surfaces of these organs, reddened more or less by some exudation from the congested vessels, through the mouth of the womb into the vagina. This menstrual, or monthly flow, marking the production of germs, and their expulsion when not fecundated by the presence of the masculine element, goes on monthly, from its commencement at the age of puberty, normally at fourteen to sixteen years of age, to the period of the cessation of the menses, or "turn of life," from forty-five to sixty, when no more germs are formed, and the capacity for child-bearing ceases.

Corresponding to the ovaries or egg-forming organs of the female, are two similar glandular bodies, called the testes, in the male, which produce the spermatic or seminal fluid, corresponding to the pollen of plants, by which the germs are fertilized, or fecundated; by means of these germ cells the masculine and feminine elements are brought together so that they can unite in the body and soul, the material and spiritual life of a new being.

Fig. 8, Upside-down cone labeled, Transverse Section through Ovary. From a case in the fifth month of pregnancy. a, b, ovarian sacs; c, ovarian ligament; d, tunica albuginea; e, stroma.
In the interior can be seen two old corpora lutea.

The testes or testicles show the importance of their function by a wonderful elaborate organization, of which some idea is given in Fig. 5, though a very imperfect one, in an ideal section intended to give an outline of the structure. The oval body is composed of a vast number of lobules, formed of very fine tubes closely folded, and everywhere in contact with blood vessels and nerves. There are in each testicle about four hundred and fifty of these lobules. The matter secreted from them passes through a vast number of tubes, 1/70 of an inch in diameter, ending in a convoluted tubular structure measuring twenty-one feet in length, ending in a single tube, which carries the masculine generative matter to the urethra, whence, in the sexual congress, it is ejected into the vagina, enters the mouth of the womb, and either there or in the Fallopian tubes, meets and impregnates the germ coming from the ovaries.

Fig. 9, Human Spermatozoa. >>

The seminal fluid is as complex and vital a substance as we should expect to have formed by so remarkable an apparatus. Floating in a liquid are minute cells, in which other cells, or corpuscles may be discovered, and in these are formed, as shown in Fig 18, bundles of spermatozoa, curiously shaped living cells, 1/600 to 1/800 in length, each one of which is furnished with a single cilium, or long slender tail, which propels it with a constant vibrative motion, as if it were a living animalcule. This

15

spermatozoon is believed to be the true agent of fertilization, corresponding to the pollen grain of the flower. It has been discovered in the womb, in the Fallopian tubes, and in contact with the germ just leaving the ovary. There can be little doubt that the cells, furnished with long propellers, as shown in Fig. 17, carry in them the male principle which gives to the female germ all that makes the child resemble its father, all that it inherits from him of bodily form, features, complexion, mental power, and moral character health, disease, idiosyncrasy; that which may make his happiness or misery in this life and who can say how much also in the life to come?

The germs of human, as of all life, are produced in immense numbers. Even in childhood imperfect germs are formed and discharged, and conception may take place before menstruation begins. Idleness, luxury, the use of rich, highly seasoned food, condiments, and stimulants, and the excitement of the passions hasten puberty, and exaggerate and disorder the corresponding masculine function.

The microscope does not reveal to us what takes place in the act of impregnation or conception, or what change is produced by the contact of the spermatozoon with the ovum. The egg of the maiden hen contains the rudiments of the chick, but it can never be hatched. The warmth that brings life and development to the impregnated egg, only hastens the putrefaction of the unimpregnated. The unimpregnated eggs of the frog quickly putrefy; but let the male element be brought soon to them, they expand into living creatures. In this case the spermatozoa can be seen becoming embedded in the gelatinous covering of the eggs, they pass through the membranes which cover them, and are probably absorbed into the ovum.

The blood goes through the testes in long, slender, tortuous arteries, presenting an extensive surface for the action of nervous energy, and there is no doubt that the best blood of the body is selected to form the semen, and that it is changed and perfected, first in these arteries and then in the wonderfully fine and convoluted tubes of the testes. The same arteries that supply blood to the testes in the male, furnish the circulation of the ovaries in the female; and the same nervous center furnishes the nerve energy and directing intelligence; but what makes the difference in action forming germ cells in one sex, and sperm cells in the other or what makes sex, must probably remain among life's inscrutable mysteries. "Arrest of development" will not account for it, and if it did, what causes arrest of development? "Male and female He created them."

At the age of puberty remarkable changes take place in both sexes. Boys and girls differ indeed from their tenderest years. As a rule boy are more boisterous, girls more gentle; while the girl chooses a doll for her plaything, the boy prefers a drum, a sword, or whip. But at puberty the sexual instincts become stronger, and there is in each a more pronounced development of masculine or feminine appearances and qualities. In the boy the voice deepens in tone, and the face begins to be covered with a beard. Where the testes have been removed, destroyed, or imperfectly developed, the voice remains treble, and the beard light or wanting. There is an enlargement of the throat, the "Adam's apple" corresponding to the full development of the masculine organs. On the other hand the girl becomes at puberty more decidedly feminine, by the enlargement of the pelvis, the broadening of the hips, and the development of the mammary or milk-forming glands in the bosom. There is no beard to mar the delicacy and feminine beauty of the face, but in both sexes alike, at this period, hair appears upon the pubes. The most striking difference, however, is that already mentioned the monthly period, marking the ripening and expulsion of germs capable of becoming living men and women.

Fig. 10, Evolution of Human Zoosperm, >>

Fig. 11, Cyst of Evolution, >>

Woman differs from man in her entire organization: mental, emotional, physical. She is more rounded, graceful, soft, sensitive, mobile. Her nervous system is finer and more delicate, with quicker sensibilities and finer powers of instinct and intuition. Even the bony skeleton of a woman can be distinguished at a glance from that of a man by its longer head and broader pelvis, and generally by its smaller hands and feet.

17

Richerand has, perhaps, exaggerated in saying the "the reproduction of the species is, in woman, the most important object in life, almost the only destination to which nature has called her, and the only duty she has to fulfil in human society;" but Madame the Stael went nearly as far in saying, "Love is but an episode in the life of man; it is the whole history of the life of woman." Byron has said almost in the same words, "Love is of man's life a thing apart; 'tis woman's whole existence."

I think, however, that there are women who have brains as well as ovaries; and that even the faculties which make women most charming as wives and most excellent as mothers, may have a much broader scope than the production, care, and education of their own offspring. Hundreds of women who have never borne children have been more than mothers to great multitudes. In the actual condition of humanity there may be a higher work for many women in saving the children of others, than in having children of their own.

CHAPTER V
Embryology

In all nature we find one singular, universal fact. All animals, without exception, high or low, of whatever ultimate complexity or simplicity of structure, originate from eggs, and from eggs of the same character. Some animals, as corals for instance, many hydroids, and other low organisms, reproduce themselves by budding or by division of the parent stock. But they also, at some time or other produce eggs, and thus bear their testimony to the general law of nature which applies to the whole animal kingdom without exception.

Fig. 12, An Ovum, >>

Indeed, the seed in plants has the same structure as the so-called ovarian egg in animals, and thus we may speak of all organized beings, vegetable or animal, as multiplying by eggs. The ovarian egg is microscopic in many animals, but whatever its size it consists of an outer bag filled with a semi-transparent fluid which is somewhat oily, and an inner bag also filled with a transparent fluid, which is chiefly albuminous. The difference in the character of the two fluids gives greater translucence to that which fills the inner sac. Within the inner bag there is a spot or dot, sometimes several of them, more or less distinct. In this condition, all eggs borne of whatever living creature, are alike.

All eggs arise in what are called ovaries. These are clusters of cells, forming bunches of a somewhat glandular character in appearance. Between these cells the eggs are formed and in such a way as at first to be hardly distinguished from the cells themselves. The same is true of sperm cells, which arise in organs of the same character as the ovary, and are formed in a manner perfectly similar to that of the formation of the egg. So we have these two spheres of growth which characterize sex in the animal kingdom, arising in conditions so very similar that the essence of the two is hardly to be determined by observation.

In order to fully appreciate what eggs are, we must remember that all organized bodies are composed of little bags which are called cells, and which are formed and multiplied in various ways.

Fig. 13, Mammal Ovum, >>
Fig. 14, Ova in the Ovary, >>
Fig. 15, Ovary and Oviduct from a laying Hen, >>
Fig. 16, Ovaries, etc., of a Bee, >>
Most of these cells are so small that they can only be perceived by the aid of high magnifying powers. There are, it is true, a few cell structures large enough to be seen with the naked eye, as, for instance, the cell of common elder pith, or the coarse cells of the orange. It is one of the great problems of modern research to ascertain how the different kinds of these cells are formed and what is their mode of reproduction. Some naturalists assume that in the animal substance secreted by a living body, such as milk which is secreted by the mammary glands, or similar substances secreted by other organs, certain particles become centers of action, around which other particles crowd; and when a little collection of this kind, microscopically small, has been formed, an envelope arises around it, and we have the *utricle* or cell. Others believe that minute, imperceptible particles of animal substance swell and enlarge, and become hollow, so that a little bag is formed, a cell envelope in short, which fills as it enlarges with a fluid substance. There are those, also, who assume that the two modes of cell formation exist simultaneously in the same being.

Fig. 17, Ideal Section of a Hen's Egg, >>
When the ovarian egg has acquired its ultimate growth, prior to the formation of the germ, the egg of the mammalia presents a bag, the so-called *zona pellucida*, the walls of which are very transparent. This bag is filled with a substance which is itself transparent, and yet which appears, under a very high magnifying power, to be granular, as if dotted with particles floating in the fluid. In that outer bag is another diminutive bag containing also a transparent fluid. The inner bag occupies an eccentric position with reference to the periphery of the outer bag, and in it are contained one or several dots. The outer envelope is called the *vitelline membrane*, because it corresponds exactly to the exceedingly thin skin inclosing the yolk in the hen's egg. The

yolk is called *vitellus*, and hence the name. The bag contains the yolk, and however transparent the fluid bay be, retains the name of yolk. The inner bag is called the germinative vesicle. The dot or dots within the germinative vesicle are ordinarily called the germinative dot or dots.

The dimensions of mammalian eggs are very small. It comes just within the range of the power of the human eye. Place the ovary under the microscope and you will find that it contains eggs of various dimensions in various stages of growth. In some the amount of yolk is less than in others; in some the germinative vesicle and the germinative dot exist; in others they are not yet formed; indeed, vesicles are found in the ovary in which neither germinative dot or germinative vesicle exists, and which are supposed to be eggs in process of formation.

If we pass now to the bird, we find in the ovary eggs which can in no way be distinguished from those observed in the ovary of the mammal, except that we find in the former a much larger number of them, and their outer envelope is much thinner. Besides those very small ovarian eggs, there are larger ones, eggs rising to dimensions so considerable that they are not only visible to the naked eye, but may be handled with facility.

Fig. 18, Egg 36 Hours after Incubation, >>

Fig. 19, Egg opened 3 Days after Incubation, >>

A mature egg in the ovary of a hen is about the dimension of a small walnut. It has no shell, no white; but it is a bulk of yolk inclosed in a vitelline membrane, containing a germinative vesicle with germinative dots. The amount of yolk is very great.

If an ovarian egg of the hen was enlarged so the germinative vesicle alone would appear as large as a whole ovarian egg at the time of maturity; we should find that the whole of the yolk consists either in little granules or in little vesicles resembling each other so much as almost to force us to the conclusion that these vesicles are only granules which have swollen and become hollow. By the side of these smaller vesicles are others somewhat larger, containing themselves a vesicle and granule; this is to say, having the true character of ordinary cells. The

21

yolk is, in fact, an accumulation of cells in various stages of growth. A large yolk, or the large ovarian egg of a hen, with its contents, was itself at one time so small as to escape the natural power of the human eye. We may place a portion of the ovary of the hen under the microscope and have at the same time in the field small eggs which cannot be seen with the naked eye, and other eggs perceptible in different degrees; and we find that the smallest are just like the eggs of mammalia, containing a transparent fluid with granules floating in it, while others contain cells already to be distinguished; and others are full of cells so large as to make the whole mass opaque. The peculiar color of the hen's egg is owing to the yellowish oil which pervades the whole substance. The study of the hen's egg in all its stages leaves no doubt that the cells at least those within the egg are formed by the swelling of the yolk particles, and their subsequent growth into larger vesicles containing a fluid, in which the elements of a perfect cell are finally matured.

Fig. 20, Unimpregnated Egg

Fig. 21, Human Egg, 2-part segmentation>>

At this stage of the ovarian egg, that is, when it has acquired vitelline membrane, germinative vesicle and germinative dot, and has also acquired certain dimensions differing in different animals, it is, or may be fecundated. This fecundation consists in the contact of sperm cells with the yolk bag.

Fig. 22, Human Egg, 4-part segmentation, >>

Fig. 23, Human Egg, further segmentation, >>

What the influence of that contact is, nobody has been able to trace. It is from that time that the changes date which lead toward the formation of a new being. But the egg of the hen, when fecundated, has not yet completed its growth. The hen's egg, as we know it, has a shell and a delicate membrane lining the shell, and a layer of white albumen surrounding the yolk. All these parts are formed after the egg has been fecundated. The egg, as we have seen, is, in its incipient condition, only an organic granule arising between the structural cells of the ovary. It grows there and acquires a remarkable complication before it has completed its successive phases as an egg. Not until it has reached the state as that of the perfect egg does it receive the contact of the spermatic cells from which dates the formation of a new being, either male or female. This in itself is a strange thing that a mother produces, not necessarily a being like herself, but quite as often beings so unlike herself in structure, as to be endowed with all the peculiarities of the male sex.

Fig. 24, The latter stages of segmentation of the human egg.

[Perimeter like Fig. 23, interior undifferentiated black.]

There is one feature in the growth of the egg of which I have as yet said nothing. The yolk, that homogeneous substance which fills the vitelline membrane, in which swim the germinative vesicle and germinative dot, must undergo a very remarkable change before it can give rise to the new individual. It is self-kneading, broken by the process of its own growth into a smaller or larger number of distinct fragments. This breaking up of the whole substance which simulates disintegration ends in a re-cementation; these fragments reunite to form the mass out of which the new germ is to be developed. This process is know as segmentation, and has been observed in the eggs of all animals. It has been studied in mammalia, in birds, in reptiles, in fishes, among articulates, among mollusks and radiates.

Fig. 25, Human Ovum, >>

Fig. 26, Human Ovum laid open, >>

This process may or may not be initiated by fecundation. There are some animals in which the first appearance of segmentation may precede fecundation; others in which it is always subsequent to fecundation; in no animal is the process known to be completed without fecundation. Neither does it take place in all animals in the same manner.

Let us take the highly magnified yolk of a mammalian egg with the germinative dots already formed on the side. The vitelline membrane surrounding such a yolk is rather thicker than in a bird's egg, and forms a sort of transparent zone outside of the yolk. When the process of segmentation begins, the yolk shrinks slightly upon itself and no longer filles the vitelline membrane completely. Presently a slight indentation becomes visible on one side of the yolk, and another corresponding to it on the opposite side. This indentation grows deeper and deeper until it cuts the yolk through, and ends in its total division in two halves, the two halves remaining, however, in close contact.

Fig. 27, Corpusclet of the Blood, >>

While this process goes on, the germinative vesicle vanishes, if indeed it has not disappeared before. In some animals the vesicle is dissolved before the segmentation begins; in others during the process. The division of the yolk in halves being completed, the same change begins now in the two halves.

Indentations are seen on either side of each half and these indentations deepen till they meet and sever the two masses of yolk; and now, where we had one yolk mass, we have four distinct lumps side by side; they become rounded in form, and look like four soft balls. The original yolk being thus divided in four, the same process goes on till the four are divided into eight, the eight into 16, the 16 into 32, the 32 into 64, and so on.

Fig. 28, Capillary Blood vessels, image undifferentiated black.

Beyond this it is almost impossible to track them individually; it is difficult to bring the whole yolk into the focus, so that each fragment can be counted, and it is pressed, however slightly, the whole mass then runs together, so that no division whatever can be traced. Occasionally however, the self-division has been followed even beyond sixty-four. By this time the yolk is transformed into a body which has much the appearance of a mulberry and this condition of the yolk has been called the mulberry stage. When it has become so far subdivided that every separate particle, owing to its diminutive size, is difficult of microscopic observation, even under very high power, each such particle seems like a cell, and may indeed be considered as a cell. This self-division of the yolk mass ends in an accumulation of cells which differ from those of the initiative yolk, and are the basis for the formation of the new being; the material in fact out of which the new being is to be built.

When conception, or the fertilization of the germ has been accomplished, a great change takes place in the system of the female, in which arises a series of functions totally unknown in the male. The ovary is quiescent. No germs are developed and expelled during the nine months of gestation; nor, normally, during the whole period of nursing. The mammary glands become active, and, in many cases, the breasts are filled with milk at an early period of pregnancy. Life flows to the bosom instead of the ovaries. As the ovarian action is suspended, there is no occasion for the menstrual excitement and evacuation. Its cessation is therefore the earliest, and, in the healthy female, the surest sign that conception has taken place. And where there is health, and the entire absence of amative excitement, as there always should be during the whole period of gestation and lactation from the beginning of pregnancy until the child is weaned the menses are suspended.

Fig. 29, Brain and Nerve>>

Foetal life has some remarkable peculiarities, which we may well consider. The formation of germs in the ovaries, their periodical development and expulsion, their impregnation or fecundation by spermatozoa formed in corresponding male organs; their extreme minuteness and rapid development into all the complexities of our wondrous organization, constitute a series of mysteries. But the mode of foetal existence is strangely different from that of the infant from the moment it comes into the world. The foetus cannot breathe. Its lungs are useless, no blood is thrown into them except what is necessary for their growth, and no air penetrates them, for the foetus swims in a liquid. The foetal heart has an open communication between the two auricles which is closed at birth. The blood of the infant gets its supply of oxygen from the blood of the mother by means of the placenta, or afterbirth. The lungs of the mother breathe for herself and her offspring during pregnancy, so that pure are is then more than ever needed.

Fig. 30, Placenta and Umbilical Cord >>

The blood of the child, fed and purified by that of the mother, passes from the placenta through the umbilical vein to its liver, and thence into the right auricle of the heart, and from that into the left auricle through the foetal opening between them, and then to the left ventricle, and is expelled into the arteries which supply the head and upper extremities with the

25

purest blood for their more rapid development. From the head and arms the blood returns into the right auricle, from which it passes to the right ventricle. In the adult it would now pass into the lungs, but in the foetus it is carried by a special artery, afterwards obliterated, into the descending aorta, and sent partly to the lower extremities, and partly to the placenta, to be purified by contact, through thin membranes, with the blood of the mother.

Here we have a special machinery, an opening in the heart which is closed at birth, lungs solid and useless, arteries and veins most important in the foetus, but at birth obliterated, and an organ expelled at birth after the infant, which in its foetal life performs the function of the stomach and lungs, furnishing the matter of blood, and also the oxygen for its purification and vivification.

Fig. 31, Embryo of the Dog, >>

There is a striking similarity of all forms of embryo. A fish, a reptile, a bird, a quadruped, a man are all vertebrates by their plan of structure and by their mode of development, and yet they are entirely distinct as members of different classes of the vertebrate type. The structural plan for all vertebrates consists of a central axis with a solid, mostly bony arch, above, inclosing the nervous system, and a similar arch below, inclosing the organs of digestion, reproduction, circulation and respiration. A glance at their embryology will show us that they are united by their development as closely as by their anatomy. Suppose we have here the egg of a vertebrate, of any vertebrate, a fish, a reptile, a bird, or a mammal; the result of the segmentation is the formation of a layer of more completely kneaded yolk substance on one side of the yolk. One end of this layer thickens more than the other. Along the middle, a slight depression is formed, not by a sinking of the center, but in consequence of the rising and swelling of the sides which leads to the formation of a kind of furrow. It is in fact only the folding upward of the upper margins; and this goes on till the margins meet and inclose a cavity. This depression in the longitudinal axis of the germ is the beginning of the arch within which the nervous system is contained. Then

26

the lower margins of the germ layer fold downward in the same way, till they also meet and form the lower cavity in which the other systems of organs are inclosed. Here a little fold occurs which is the first sketching out of the eye; here another fold, the first indication of the ear; here transverse fissures are developed which are to be the gills; for gills exist in all vertebrates, including man, in the embryonic state. As the development goes on, the germ rises more and more above the yolk, the connection becomes less and less, the yolk hangs like a bag below the body, and either is slowly or more rapidly absorbed into it, as the case may be in different vertebrates, and the little animal is finally freed from all connection with the parent. Compare a number of vertebrates from different classes in different stages of growth, and you will be astonished at their great resemblance. Take them, for instance, at an early stage of embryonic life, before the germ rises very high above the yolk. At that time blood-vessels extend over the whole yolk, some of which bring the blood to the heart, while others distribute it to all parts of the surface. At this point of the developments there are two great vessels from which the blood circulates symmetrically on either side of the body, while both finally unite in a circular vessel. Whether we take a turtle, a snake, a bird, or a mammal at this phase of development, the difference in their circulation is very slight. Only very careful and detailed drawings, such as are here reproduced from the works of Rathke, Tander, Bischoff, and Agassiz, give it to you.

The body of the snake is hardly more elongated than that of the turtle; the form tapers into a tail in both, but not more in one than in the other. A young fish exhibits the same traits of physiognomy which we observe as characteristic of the embryo of the reptiles, the birds or the mammalia. There is, in fact, no more difference between these different embryos, than between the young star fish, the young jelly fish, and the young coral. The Vertebrates, like the Radiates, pass through an uninterrupted series of changes from the first formation of the germ to the completion of its growth, which are throughout parallel to one another. How, then, does it come that the germ of a turtle always produces a turtle, the germ of a snake always a snake, the germ of a dog always a dog, the germ of a man always a human being, if there be not something superior to these physical resemblances controlling all growth throughout the civilized world.

CHAPTER VI.
Pregnancy--Labor--Parturition.

Perhaps there is no more eventful period in the history of woman than that in which she first becomes conscious that the existence of another being is dependent upon her own, and that she carries about with her the first tiny rudiments of an immortal soul.

The signs of pregnancy are various. Many females are troubled with colic pains, creeping of the skin, shuddering, and fainting fits immediately on conception taking place. Where such symptoms occur immediately after connection, they are a certain indication of impregnation.

A remarkable change takes place in the face in most cases, varying in time from three days to three months. The eyes are dull and heavy, and present a glassy appearance the nose pinched up, the skin becomes pale and livid, and the whole countenance appears as if five or ten years advance in life had been taken at a single step.

Another important and remarkable sign, and one the most to be relied on, is an increase of the size of the neck. This often occurs at a very early period, and many females, by keeping a careful daily measurement of the neck, can always tell when they are pregnant.

A suppression of the menstrual flow is another strong presumptive sign. It is true, a partial flow of the menses often occurs after pregnancy, from the lower part of the womb, but when the flow is suddenly stopped without any apparent cause, pregnancy is generally the predisposing cause.

Soon after conception, the stomach often becomes affected with what is called morning sickness. On first awaking the female feels as well as usual, but on rising from her bed qualmishness begins, and perhaps while in the act of dressing, retching and vomiting takes place.

This symptom may occur almost immediately after conception; but it most frequently commences for the first time between two and three weeks after. Now and then it is experi-

29

enced only the last six weeks or two months of pregnancy, when it is attended generally with much distress and discomfort. It continues, more or less, during the first half of pregnancy, and subsides about the time the movements of the child begin to be felt.

Changes in the breast are generally considered as strong signs of pregnancy. When two months of pregnancy have been completed, an uneasy sensation of throbbing and stretching fullness is experienced, accompanied with tingling about the middle of the breasts, centering in the nipples. A sensible alteration in their appearance soon follows they grow larger and more firm. The nipple becomes more prominent, and the circle around its base altered in color and structure, constituting what is called the areola; and, as pregnancy advances, milk is secreted.

The period of gestation, at which these changes may occur, varies much in different females. Sometimes, with the exception of the secretion of the milk, they are recognized very soon after conception; in other instances, particularly in females of a weakly and delicate constitution, they are hardly perceptible until pregnancy is far advanced, or even drawing toward its termination.

The changes in the form and size of the breast may be the result of causes unconnected with pregnancy. They may enlarge in consequence of marriage, from the individual becoming stout and fat, or from accidental suppression of the monthly flow.

The changes which take place in the nipple and around its base, are of the utmost value as an evidence of pregnancy.

About the sixth or seventh week after conception has taken place, if the nipple be examined, it will be found becoming turgid and prominent, and a circle forming around its base, of a color deeper in its shade than rose or flesh color, slightly winged with a yellow or brownish line, and here and there upon its surface will be seen little prominent points from about ten to twenty in number. In the progress of the next six or seven more weeks these changes are fully developed, the nipple becoming more prominent and turgid than ever, the circle around it of larger dimensions, the skin being soft, bedewed with a slight degree of moisture, frequently staining the linen in contact with it; the little prominences of larger size, and the color of the whole very much deepened.

Calculations of the duration of pregnancy, founded upon what has been observed after casual intercourse, or perhaps a single act, in individuals who can have no motive to tell us what is false, are likely to be correct. The conclusion drawn from these is, that labor usually, but not invariably, comes on about 280 days after conception, a mature child being sometimes born before the expiration of the forty weeks, and at other times not until that time had been exceeded by several days. A case is on record where the pregnancy existed 287 days. In this case, the labor did not take place until that period had elapsed from the departure of the husband for the East Indies, consequently the period might have been longer than 287 days.

Childbirth is a natural process, and however complicated and painful habits or disease have made it, yet the work must be left to Nature. Any efforts to assist or hurry matters will only end in harm. The only cases where interference is justifiable is where her powers are exhausted, or some malformation exists or mal-presentation occurs. When labor is about to commence, the womb descends into the bottom of the belly, and the motions and weight of the child will be felt much lower down than usual. If in a natural position, the head will fall down to the mouth of the womb, and press upon it. This drives forward the membranes which retain the water at the orifice, and at the proper moment they break, and labor then commences.

Labor is caused by involuntary contraction of the uterus and abdominal muscles. By their force the *liquor amnii* flows out, the head of the foetus is engaged in the pelvis, it goes through it, and soon passes out by the vulva, the folds of which disappear. The different phenomena take place in succession, and continue a certain time; they are accompanied with pains more or less severe, with swelling and softening of the soft parts of the pelvis and external genital parts, and with an abundant mucous secretion in the cavity of the vagina. All these circumstances, each in its own way, favor the passage of the foetus.

It is proper here to remark that parturition is not necessarily either painful or dangerous. It is well known that women in an uncivilized state suffer very little pain or disablement in bringing forth children, generally neither pregnancy or labor iterrupt the ordinary avocation of the mother, except for an hour or two at the birth itself. The suffering and debilitating influences that often attend child-birth now, are caused by our unnatural modes of living, and non-attention to the laws of health. Numerous well authenticated instances are known, where women, who had previously suffered with severe labor in childbirth, have, by attention to health and diet as here indicated, been delivered of fine health children with comparative ease.

From the beginning of pregnancy, more than ordinary care should be used in taking regular exercise in the open air, being careful to avoid fatigue and over-exertion; during the whole period of pregnancy every kind of agitating exercise, such as running, jumping, jolting in a carriage, dancing, lifting heavy weights, and plunging in cold water, should be carefully avoided, as well as the passions being kept under perfect control.

The diet must chiefly consist of fruits and farinacious food, as sago, tapioca, rice, &c. In proportion as a woman subsists on aliment free from earthy and boney matter, will she avoid pain and danger in delivery; hence the more ripe fruit, acid fruit in particular, and the less of other kinds of food, but particularly of bread or pastry of any kind, is consumed, the less will be the danger on sufferings of child-birth. Nearly all kinds of fruit possess two hundred times less ossifying principle than bread, or anything else made of wheaten flour.

Honey, molasses, sugar, butter, oil, vinegar, etc., when unadulterated, are entirely free from earth matter. Common salt, pepper, coffee, cocoa, spices, and many drugs are much worse than wheaten flour, in their hardening and bone-forming tendency, and should therefore be avoided. The drink should be tea or lemonade made with water, soft and clear, and, where practicable, distilled.

No mother who has adopted this mode of living, but has

blessed the knowledge of it, and it has saved many a young mother much needless terror.

CHAPTER VII.
Love and Marriage.

The attraction of the sexes for each other, though based upon the dual principle of generation which pervades the living world, and which has its analogies in the attractive forces of matter, yet pervades the whole being. Love is not merely the instinctive desire of physical union, which has for its object the continuation of the species; it belongs to the mind as well as the body; it warms, invigorates, and elevates every sentiment, every feeling, and in its highest, purest, most diffusive form, unites us to God, and all creatures in Him.

All love is essentially the same, but modified according to its objects, and by the character of the one who loves. The love of children for their parents, of parents for offspring, brotherly and sisterly love, the love of friendship, of charity, and the fervor of religious love, are modifications of the same sentiment, the attraction that draws us to our kindred, our kind that binds together all races, and humanity itself, resting on the Fatherhood of God, and the brotherhood of man. It is but natural that this love should vary in degrees. Attractions are proportional to proximity. Family is nearer than country; we prefer our own nation to the rest of the race.

Each individual has also his own special attraction and repulsions. There is love at first sight, and friendship at first sight. We feel some persons pleasant to us; to be near them is a delight. Generally such feelings are mutual, like flows to like; or, as often, perhaps, differences fit into each other. We seek sympathy with our own tastes and habits; or we find in others what we lack. Thus the weak rest upon the strong, the timid are fond of the courageous, the reckless seek guidance of the prudent, and so on.

The sentiment of love for the opposite sex tender, romantic, passionate, begins very early in life. Fathers and daughters, mothers and sons, have a special fondness for each other, as also have brothers and sister; but the boy soon comes to admire someone, generally older than himself who is not a relation.

Very little girls find a hero in some friend of an elder brother. Fondness for cousins generally comes more from opportunity than natural attraction, though a cousin may have very little appearance of family relation. The law appears to be that free choice seeks the diverse and distant. A stranger has always a better chance with the young ladies of any district than the young men with whom they have always been acquainted. Savages seek their wives out of their own tribes.

It is my belief that, naturally, I mean in a state of pure and unperverted nature, but developed, cultivated and refined by education, every man loves womanhood itself and all women so far as they approximate to his ideal; and that, in the same way, every woman loves manhood, and is attracted and charmed by all its gently, noble, and heroic manifestations. By such a man, every woman he meets is reverenced as a woman, accepted as a friend, loved as a mother, sister, daughter, or it may be, cherished in a more tender relation, which should be at first, and may always remain, pure and free from any sensual desire. Such love may have many objects, each attracting the kind and degree of affection which it is able to inspire. Such love of men for women, and women for men, may be free, and will be free, just in the degree in which it is freed from the bondage of sensual passion. Such love has a direct tendency to raise men above the control of their senses. The more such love one has, and the more it is diffused, the less the liability to sink into the lower and disorderly loves of the sensual life.

The idea that every attraction, every attachment, every love between the sexes, must lead to marriage, that no love can be tolerated but with that end in view, is a false and mischievous one. It deprives men and women of the strength and happiness they might have in pure friendships and pure loves, and it leads to a multitude of false and bad marriages. Two persons are drawn together by strong attractions and tender sentiments for each other, who have no more right to be married than if they were brother and sister, but who have the same right to love each other. But their true sentiments for each other, and consequent

35

relation to each other, are not understood by those around them, and perhaps not by themselves. They are urged, by the misapprehension of others, by their expectation, by ignorant gossip, by the prejudice of society based upon low and sensual estimates of life, to marry; they find often that they must either marry or lose the happiness they have in each other's society, and they make the irrevocable mistake.

When it is understood that there are other loves than that of marriage when the special attraction that justifies union for life, and the begetting of offspring, is discriminated from all the other attractions that may bring two souls into very near and tender relations to each other, there will be more happiness in the world, and fewer incomplete, imperfect, and therefore more or less unhappy marriages. Nothing can be more detestable than playing with fire, which goes by the name of flirtation; but there are men and women who have the happiness of loving, and of being tenderly and devotedly loved, by persons of the opposite sex--loved purely, nobly, and happily, without injury, and with great good. Where such loves are accompanied by perfect trust in the goodness, purity, truth, and honor of the beloved, there can be no jealousy no desire for selfish absorption no fear of deprivation of any right. There is no reason why a husband or wife should limit the range of pure and spiritual affections to near relatives. The man who can love a sister or sisters, may love in the same way, or as purely, a woman who might be his sister. As men and women learn to purify their lives, the world will grow more tolerant, and love will become more universal. The tender and fervent exhortations to mutual love, to be found in the Gospels and Epistles of the New Testament, are now almost without a meaning. But they had a meaning to those to whom they were addressed, and when we are better Christians, and bring our lives to the purity of Christian morality, they will have a meaning to us, and we shall learn that in a sense we have not dreamed of, God is Love.

In the human race all circumstances point to monogamy as the law, or natural condition. Males and females are born in almost exactly equal numbers. If there are two or three per cent.

more of males than females, the risks of life with males soon make the number even. Therefore, as a rule, no man can have more than one wife without robbing his neighbor. Polygamy is therefore a manifest injustice, and may become the most grievous of all monopolies.

Children are the most helpless of all young creatures, and require the care of parents for the longest period. The care of a husband for his wife, and of a father for his child, is an evident necessity. The proper care and education of a single child should extend over at least fifteen years, and that of a family may reach to thirty years, or throughout the greater part of an ordinary life. During all periods of pregnancy, child-bearing, nursing, and the education and care of a family, every woman has the right to the sympathy, sustaining love, and constant aid of her husband. No man has the right to desert or leave helpless, or even dependent upon others, except in extraordinary cases, the mother of his children.

Marriage, like celibacy, should be a matter of vocation. The special object of marriage is to have children the co-operating motive is that two persons, drawn to each other by mutual affection, may live helpfully and happily together. A self-ish marriage for its merely animal gratifications, a marriage in which strength, health, usefulness, often life itself are sacrificed to sensuality and lust is a desecration of a holy institution, and somewhat worse in its consequences than promiscuous profligacy, for the consequences of that may not fall upon one's children and posterity.

There are many persons who have no right to marry. There should be a kind and amount of love that will justify and sanctify such a relation. There should be a pure motive, and a fixed intention of making the relation what it ought to be to husband, wife, and children. There should be a reasonable assurance of the power to provide for a family. There should be that amount of health, that freedom from bodily and mental disease, that physical and moral constitution which will give a reasonable prospect of children whose lives will be a blessing to themselves and to society.

Where there is deformity of body or an unhappy peculiarity of mind or temper liable to be inherited, people should not marry, or if they live together, should resign the uses of marriage. People should conscientiously refrain from propagating hereditary diseases. Persons near of kin are wisely forbidden to marry, for there is in such cases the liability of imperfect generation the production of blind, deaf, idiotic or insane offspring. Should marriage be for life? As a rule, undoubtedly. Every real, proper, true marriage must be. It takes a lifetime for a husband and wife to make a home, and rear, and educate, and provide for a family of children. But how if people make mistakes and find that they are not suitably married? These are mistakes very difficult to remedy. If a man, after deliberately making his choice of a woman, ceases to love her, how can he honorably withdraw from his relation to her, and enter upon another, when she still loves him, and is ready to fulfill her part of the contract? Laws cannot very well provide for mistakes. If the distaste for each other be mutual, and both parties desire to separate, a separation may of course be permitted, but it is a serious question whether two such persons can go into the world and find new partners, with justice to the rest. The law which permits of no divorce certainly bears hard upon individual cases, but if it leads to greater seriousness and care in forming such relation, it may be, on the whole, the best thing for society that it should be strictly observed.

CHAPTER VIII
When to Marry--
How to Select a Partner on Right Principles.

The proper age to marry is a somewhat vexing question, but needlessly so, because that age varies much, according to temperament and other circumstances relating to the individual. Although, after puberty, the sexual organs are capable of reproduction, yet it by no means follows that they should be used for that purpose. Their early activity is intended for the perfection of the body and mind, and not for the continuation of the species. Very early marriages, therefore, should be avoided, because the nervous force expended in amative inulgence is imperatively required in both sexes, for developing the physical and mental faculties. The zoo-spermes produced by the male in the first years of puberty are inferior in power, and less capable of producing healthy offspring than those of maturer years. The early germs, also, of the female are less fitted for fecundation than those that appear later in life. Nature evidently intending these early efforts to be used on the individuals themselves, in buiding up their bodies, strengthening their minds, and preparing them to reproduce their species in maturer years. There is a serious day of reckoning for early indulgence; for precocious persons--unless their constitutions are as powerful as their desires--who give way to their passions at their first exactions, barter their youth for their enjoyment, and are old and weary of the world at an age when people of more moderate habits are only in the meridian of pleasure and existence.

Generally, the best age to marry, where the health is perfect, is from twenty-one to twenty-five in the male, and from eighteen to twenty-one in the female. As a general rule, marriages earlier than this are injurious and detrimental to health. Men who marry too young, unless they are of cold and phlegmatic constitutions, and thus moderate in their conduct, become partially bald, dim of sight, and lose all elasticity of limb, in a few years; while women, in a like position, rarely have any bloom on ther cheek or fire in their eye, by the time they are twenty-five. And all profound physiologists agree that, from the same cause, the mental faculties suffer in the same ratio.

A medium, however, is to be observed. It is not well to defer till middle age the period of connubial intercourse; for too tedious spinstership is as much calculated to hasten the decay of beauty, as too early a marriage. Hence, there is rarely any freshness to be seen in a maiden of thirty; while the matron of that age, if her life has been a happy one, and her hymenial condition of not more than ten years' standing, is scarcely in the hey-day of her charms. And the same rule will apply with equal force to the other sex; for, after the first prime of life, bachelors decay and grow old much faster than married men.

The rich are qualified for marriage before the poor. This is owing to the superiority of their aliment; for very nutritious food, and the constant use of wines, coffee, etc., greatly assist in developing the organs of reproduction; whereas the food generally made use of among the peasantry of most countries, such as vegetables, corn, milk, etc., retards their growth. Owing to this difference of diet, the daughter of a man of wealth, who keeps a good table, will be as adequate to certain duties of married life at eighteen, as the daughter of a humble peasant at twenty-one. Singular as it may seem, it is none the less true, that love-novels, amorous conversations, playing parlor games for kisses, voluptuous pictures, waltzing, and in fact, all things having a tendency to create desire, assist in promoting puberty, and preparing young persons for early marriage. Those who reach this estate, however, by artificial means, and much before the natural period, will have to suffer for it in after-life.

The female who marries before the completion of her womanhood that is, before her puberty is established will cease to grow, and probably become pale and delicate; the more especially if she becomes pregnant soon after marriage. A person who is thus circumstanced, will also be liable to abortions, and painful deliveries. Marriage, unless under very peculiar circumstances, should not take place until two or three years after the age of puberty. Many instances could be cited of the injurious effects resulting from not observing this rule. The case of the son of Napoleon I. is a notable instance, who at the age of fifteen or sixteen, began his career of sexual indulgence, which ended his life at the early age of twenty-one years. He was an amiable, inoffensive, and studious youth beloved by his grandfather and the whole Austrian Court; and though the son of the most energetic man that modern times has produced, yet, from his effeminate life, he scarcely attracted the least public attention.

Let me, therefore advise the male reader to keep his desires in leading strings until he is at least twenty-one, and the female not to enter within the pale of wedlock until she is past her eighteenth year; but after those periods marriage is their proper sphere of action, and one in which they must play a part or suffer actual pain, as well as the loss of one of the greatest of earthly pleasures.

Marriages are most happy, and most productive of handsome and healthy offspring, when the husband and wife differ, not only in mental conformation, but in bodily construction. A melancholy man should mate himself with a sprightly woman, and vice versa; for otherwise they will soon grow weary of the monotony of each other's company. By the same rule should the choleric and the patient be united, and the ambitious and the humble; for the opposites of their natures not only produce pleasurable excitement, but each keeps the other in a wholesome check. In the size and form of the parties, the same principles hold good. Tall women are not the ideals of beauty to tall men; and if they marry such, they will soon begin to imagine greater perfections in other forms than in those of their own wives. And this is well ordered by Nature, to prevent the disagreeable results which are almost certain to grow out of unions where the parties have a strong resemblance.

For instance: tall parents will probably have children taller than either, and mental imbecility is the usual attendant of extreme size. The union of persons prone to corpulency, of dwarfs, etc. would have parallel results; and so, likewise, of weakly or attenuated couples. The tall should marry the short the corpulent the lean the choleric the gentle and so on; and the tendency to extremes in the parents will be corrected in the offspring.

Apart from these considerations, there are reasons why persons of the same disposition should not be united in wedlock. An amiable wife to a choleric man, is like oil to troubled waters; an ill-tempered one will make his life a misery and his home a hell. The man of studious habits should marry a woman of sense and spirit rather than of erudition, or the union will increase the monotony of his existence, which it would be well for his health and spirits to correct by a little conjugal excitement; and the man of gloomy temperament will find the greatest relief from the dark forebodings of his mind in the society of a gentle, but lively and smiling partner.

However, in some particulars the dispositions and construction of married people must assimilate, or they will have but few enjoyments in common. The man of full habits and warm nature had better remain single than unite his destinies with a woman whose heart repulses the soft advancements of love; and the sanguine female, in whose soul love is the dominant principle, should avoid marriage with a very phlegmatic person, or her caresses instead of being returned in kind, will rather excite feeling of disgust. Thus the discriminations to be made in the choice of a partner are extremely nice.

Nature generally assists Art in the choice of partners. We instinctively seek in the object of our desires the qualities which we do not possess ourselves. this is a most admirable arrangement of Providence, as it establishes an equilibrium, and prevents people from tending to extremes; for it is known that unions of dwarfs are fruitful of dwarfs; that giants proceed from the embrace of giants; and that the offspring of parents alike irritable, alike passive, alike bashful, etc., inherit the prominent qualities of both to such a degree as to seriously interfere with their prospects in the world.

It has another advantage. Through its means "every eye forms its own beauty," what one person rejects is the beau ideal of another's conception; thus we are all provided for.

In fine, with man as with animals, the best way to improve the breed is to cross it, for the intermarriage of like with like, and relative with relative, not only causes man to degenerate, but if the system became universal, would in time bring the human race to a termination altogether.

A male or female with a very low forehead should carefully avoid marriage with a person of like conformation, or their offspring will, in all probability, be weak-minded, or victims to partial idiocy.

The system of crossing is so perfect, that marriages between persons, natives of different countries, are likely to be pleasant and fruitful. Speaking on this subject an English writer says:

"The Persians have been so improved by introducing foreigners to breed from, that they have completely succeeded in washing out the stain of their Mongolian origin."

And the same author adds to the effect, that in those parts of Persia where there is no foreign intercourse, the inhabitants are sickly and stunted; while in those that are frequented by strangers, they are large and healthy.

To make what is called a "handsome couple," the female should be about three inches less than the male; and the parties should be proportionably developed throughout their system.

"A well-formed woman," says a modern physiologist, "should have her head, shoulder, and chest small and compact; arms and limbs relatively short; her haunches apart; her hips elevated; her abdomen large, and her thighs voluminous. Hence, she should taper from the center up and down. Whereas, in a well-formed man the shoulders are more prominent than the hips. Great hollowness of the back, the pressing of the thighs against each other in walking, and the elevation of one hip above the other, are indications of the malformations of the pelvis."

From the same writer I take the following, which is applicable here. It is very correct in its estimates of beauty in both sexes.

"The length of the neck should be proportionably less in the male than in the female, because the dependence of the mental system on the vital one is naturally connected with the shorter courses of the vessels of the neck.

"The neck should form a gradual transition between the body and the head its fullness concealing all prominences of the throat.

"The shoulders should slope from the lower part of the neck, because the reverse shows that the upper part of the chest owes its width to the bones and muscles of the shoulders.

"The upper part of the chest should be relatively short, and wide, independent of the size of the shoulders, for this shows the vital organs which it contains are sufficiently developed.

"The waist should taper little farther than the middle of the trunk, and be marked, especially in the back and loins, by the approximation of the hips.

"The waist should be narrower than the upper part of the trunk and its muscles, because the reverse indicates the expansion of the stomach, liver, and great intestines, resulting from their excessive use.

"The back of woman should be more hollow than that of man; for otherwise the pelvis is not of sufficient depth for parturition.

"Woman should have loins more extended than man, at the expense of the superior and inferior parts, for this conformation is essential to gestation.

"The abdomen should be larger in woman than in man, for the same reason.

"Over all these parts, the cellular tissue, and the plumpness connected with it, should obliterate all distinct projection of muscles.

"The surface of the whole female form should be characterized by its softness, elasticity, smoothness, delicacy and polish, and by the gradual and easy transition between the parts.

"The moderate plumpness already described should bestow on the organs of the woman great suppleness.

"Plumpness is essential to beauty, especially in mothers, because in them the abdomen necessarily expand, and would afterwards collapse and become wrinkled.

"An excess of plumpness, however, is to be guarded against. Young women who are very fat are cold, and prone to barrenness. In no case should plumpness be so predominant as to destroy the distinctness of parts.

"A male or female formed on the above models would be well matched and have fine children."

CHAPTER IX
A Special Chapter to Young Men, Upon a Special Subject.

I desire, young men, to enlist your earnest attention in what I now say; its proper consideration, will determine in a great measure, the character of your future career. You have now arrived at that age, when you have in a large degree to act on your own responsibility, and take your place as a worker in the world's progress. Your childhood being passed away, your parents, friends and society now look upon you and expect you to assume your allotted portion of work as a means of securing a livelihood. No one who has health has any right to existence without doing work of some kind. To help you to fill your sphere happily, successfully and worthily, has been my object in writing this chapter. No young man who has evinced a desire for the companionship of prostitutes has ever succeeded in the end, no matter what advantages he may have had in the way of friends, fortune or talents.

I take it for granted you profess Christianity, and believe in a heaven and a hell, or a future state of rewards and punishments, according to the deeds done in the body.

To the atheist or the professional profligate, who acknowledges no law, human or divine, I do not address myself. I leave him in the hands of the living God, who will surely call him to account when he least expects it.

You find yourself in the enjoyment of life, health and strength, inhabiting a beautiful world, and surrounded by abundant means of delight and happiness; and you know, not only that you did not give yourself this life, but that you are utterly powerless to prolong it even for an instant; in fact, that you are momentarily dependent for life and all its blessings on its Divine Giver. This consideration need not in the least prevent you from the unrestrained pursuit of any innocent pleasures; but it should lead you to be most careful to abstain from any of an opposite character.

When a mere boy you preferred the companionship of boys, and probably scorned or were ashamed to play with girls.

46

Now on the contrary, you feel yourself powerfully attracted towards young women; and find yourself much happier in their company than in the company of young men. Whence, think you, comes this remarkable change? Is it not from Him who is the only Source of life and love, and who, in His wisdom and mercy, has made the two sexes, and made them for each other: and what could be His motive in this but the desire to promote the eternal happiness of His creatures? It is, too, by this wise and beneficent provision that He secures the perpetuation of the human race in this world, and a continual addition to the host of good men made perfect in His happy kingdom above.

This new feeling you may take as a notice from God that the time is approaching when it will behoove you to look about for a maiden whom you can love with a pure affection, and whom you believe you can make happy as your wife. Attend to the voice of God thus addressed to you; or, take the consequences.

God, as we see, has not made us angels at once, but has placed us in this world of probation, where, associated with our fellows of various and conflicting dispositions and interests, we may form our character, and be gradually prepared for our eternal home. To assist us in this preparation, and to guide us in our course of action, we often need the counsels of a judicious and kind friend; and in this case one of our own sex may be, and often is, highly valuable. But at times there are peculiar circumstances when one of the other sex, a better half, to whom we can without reserve unbosom ourselves is beyond all comparison preferable. To each sex God has given qualities suited to meet the wants as well as to enhance the joys, of the other.

Every right-minded young man, on attaining a suitable age, desires to become a husband and a father; and the prospect cheers him in his toil, and nerves his arm to greater and more persistent labor than he would be willing to undertake for himself alone. He is looking forward to provide for others far dearer to him than himself.

Now, as God knows all things, He knows what pairs are fitted for each other; indeed, we cannot doubt that He provides them. But the world is in a fallen state I think you will cordially agree with me here and consequently it is often difficult, or almost impossible, for any of us to know who are the right parties to come together.

Suppose, however, by some extraordinary means, you should happen to know what maiden would become your wife, what would be your thoughts and feelings if without marriage, she were previously, for a time however short, to live with another man? Would you not think her defiled and unworthy of you? Do not most men take the same view? How then, think you can any accountable being be willing to defile a woman that is to be the wife of another?

If you are right-minded you will, in the first place, seek for purity in your bride; and if you are honest, and worthy of a wife, you will take especial care not to be her inferior in that respect.

The Almighty Creator, in His love and mercy towards His creatures, permits them to co-operate with Him in continuing His creation; and hence flow all the endearing affections and relationships of home and family.

The lawful love of man for woman, and of woman for man, is the best and holiest affection of which our nature is susceptible; it is also the strongest and the most enduring, and, as it proceeds from God Himself, nothing can be more certain that the orderly compliance with its dictates secures health and happiness here and hereafter; while, on the other hand, the abuse of this love as certainly entails the loss of all self-respect, and, unless repented of, eternal woe.

A man who has been guilty of fornication may afterwards desire to contract marriage, and with that view may pay his addresses to a respectable, modest young woman; but can he knowing, as he must, his own character do so without a feeling of inferiority, shame, and remorse? Assuming that he has seen and repented of his wicked folly, he ought, before taking such a step, to perform a mental quarantine, say of not less than six months; in other words, he ought for a considerable time, to abstain not only from lascivious acts and practices, but also from

48

encouraging unchaste thoughts, so as to have a well-grounded assurance that he has effectually abandoned his vicious practices, and is determined for the future to pursue a virtuous course, such as may become a Christian husband and father.

Supposing you have a sister whom you tenderly love, and some man perhaps a friend of yours should by taking advantage of her unsuspecting credulity, succeed in seducing her, you would doubtless consider him an unprincipled villain, and deserving of the most condign punishment. If too, as is often the case, she should in consequence, although unmarried, become a mother, you know the disgrace into which she would fall, especially in the eyes of her own sex. Parents, in such cases, not unfrequently turn their backs on the child they had tenderly reared, and from whose honorable marriage they had expected a large addition to their own happiness. But suppose the victim, instead of being your sister, were only an acquaintance, or even a stranger, would not your detestation of the villainy be quite as real, though perhaps not so intense?

In all such cases and alas! They are far too numerous, the evil is one of the greatest that can befall a human being; and, although the men commonly go scatheless in the eyes of the world, are they not in the eyes of God, who alone judges rightly as truly and lamentably fallen as the women?

In the three commandments, forbidding murder, adultery, and theft, I remark that adultery is placed between the other two; and from this I infer that the crime of the adulterer lies somewhere between that of a murderer and a thief. For does not adultery to which fornication is the natural stepping-stone partake of the nature of both murder and theft? To deprive a woman of her chastity is robbery of the basest description; and adultery injures or destroys the soul as certainly as poison does the body. To me it appears that the phrase, a Christian murderer, a Christian adulterer, a Christian thief, or a Christian drunkard, is a contradiction in terms; and that so long as such a character attaches to any one he is unchristianized, self-excommunicated, and utterly disqualified for heaven.

Let me here, however, add that I firmly believe there is

such a thing as genuine repentance; and therefore that any one who has committed a crime, however heinous, may repent, and so become fitted for admission to the pure society in heaven. But I know full well that real repentance is both difficult and rare; and therefore how extremely dangerous it is for any one to enter on a vicious course.

It is often easy enough to evade man's laws; indeed, not a few of them are more honored in the breach than in the observance. Being in their very nature imperfect, they are liable to and admit of alteration and improvement. God's laws, however, are the reverse of all this. They are perfect and unalterable in their nature, and all intended and calculated to promote our good, are certain in their effects, and eternal in their operation, like Him who gave them; and, happily, there is no escape from them. This important fact is forgotten or neglected whenever we knowingly give way to any vicious propensity. As we sow we are certain to reap.

In my view, it is according to God's law that a man should attach himself to one woman in that most intimate relation, Marriage, and one woman to one man, ever being careful not to do anything that would divert the affections of any one from their proper object; for to each one God has given a right to one, and only one. It is our duty jealously to guard our own right; and, if our practice conform to our Christian profession, we shall be as careful, to the utmost of our power, not to infringe the rights of other, especially on this most tender point. Whoever, then, commits fornication or adultery, trespasses on the domain of another, and so offends God's law, and must inevitably take the consequences; and, recollect, the punishment that naturally follows any wicked act is ever in exact proportion to its atrocity.

Whatever some may think or say, do not you give heed to the notion that 'A reformed rake makes the best husband.' Many a youth may have fancied that he might, with little or no danger, have just a taste of intoxicating liquor, or of fornication, and give it up after a time; forgetting that practice makes perfect as well in a bad cause as a good one and that a habit once acquired is very rarely got rid of: witness the number of confirmed drunkards, and permanently diseased and decayed libertines, sunk to the lowest depths of degradation. How is it, I wonder, that we do not hear it said 'A reformed harlot makes the best wife?' Reform is surely as possible for women as for men. I hope and believe that many harlots do repent and reform; but I fear a very great many more do not: for it is well known that those who have once fallen into a vicious practice, whatever it may be, are far more in danger of repeating it than those who have never entered upon it.

I am well aware that young men are liable to be tempted to stray from the path of duty in a great variety of ways, some of them insidious and dangerous. Many have large sums of money passing through their hands, or large stocks of valuable goods, some of which they might easily take with but little chance of detection; yet they safely pass through the trying ordeal. Sometimes they will be invited by their youthful acquaintances, of either sex, to partake of pleasures which their conscience tells them are anything but innocent. In all such cases, let them as zealously guard their own chastity as they habitually do their employer's property; and they will at the same time promote their own welfare, and do something towards bettering the condition of the world.

A casual visitor to our casinos, music-halls, and other places where loose girls and fast young men do congregate, might fancy there was no harm going on, that all was innocent amusement; but could he follow a portion of the company when the closing time arrives, he would have great reason to change his opinion. Some of the less cautious, having drunk too freely, soon find their way to the cells of the police station; but the greater number indulge their lustful propensities in dens of infamy where they are pretty safe from interference.

Indulgence in fornication inevitably entails no little expense often much more than would support a family in comfort and respectability; and whence, think you, are the funds supplied? Doubtless from some channel that should have a different and a better destination; and, when ordinary sources fail, an employer's till or cash-box, or his cheque-book is not

51

unfrequently resorted to. Detection may not immediately follow, and the downward course is pursued till, from the magnitude of the robbery, or perhaps trifling circumstances, it can no longer be concealed, and at one blow, a felon's fate puts an end to the dissipation and forever blasts the prospects of the infatuated youth.

Like other vices, fornication is progressive in its nature, and has the most lamentable consequences. As petty theft is a stepping stone to burglary, and indulgence in drink to habitual drunkenness and delirium tremens, so fornication, when once entered on, may lead to adultery, and that may provoke homicide which, under the circumstances, would be deemed justifiable, as a jury would assert by their verdict; or it may lead to divorce and bring disgrace and wretchedness to a number of innocent people and children.

One of the saddest results of fornication is the immense number of illegitimate children that are brought into the world, and who have not that parental care which they so much need, and to which they are so justly entitled.

How often young women are charged with the murder of their infants; and, although it is almost certain they are guilty of that crime, they are convicted only of concealing the birth. Who can tell the mental anguish they must have endured ere they could make up their minds to destroy their babes? In truth, it is quite enough to bring on temporary insanity, and so to justify the merciful verdict. Very probably, too, several of the jury felt self-convicted of having participated in a similar, though undiscovered, crime. In these cases, who will say that the fathers of those little innocents are less guilty than the wretched and disgraced mothers?

All vices carry their punishment with them, and this, too, with unerring certainty, although it does not always follow them swiftly. To this, which is one of God's laws, fornication is no exception. A young man may, perchance, practice it for some time with apparent impunity; or he may, on the other hand unhappily, as he will doubtless consider it at once contract a disease so loathsome that he dares not avow it, but strives to conceal it; and so virulent, that it may either carry him to an early grave, or, after the doctors have done their best for him, leave him debilitated for life, a burden to himself and others. Unlike other diseases, this is deemed unfit to be spoken of in decent society; indeed, it is never alluded to, and is therefore more likely to be neglected till it has so thoroughly got hold of the system that recovery is hopeless. The sinning women, too, are equally subject to this horrible curse. Whole wards in our hospitals and lunatic asylums are filled with its victims. Such, however, is but the natural punishment which a merciful God permits to follow a violation or abuse of one of His most beneficent laws; by this means plainly showing us the grievous nature of the crime. If the terrible character, and the inevitable certainty of this natural consequence of the act were known in time, it ought to be sufficient to deter any young person from vicious courses. Forewarned they would be forearmed.

In order to be convinced of the direful evils resulting from this vice, we need only look at the swarms of prostitutes that infest all our large centres of population; and, truth to tell, in proportion to their size, our villages and quiet hamlets are no less immoral. Most of these unfortunates, and their male associates too, pass much of their time in riotous enjoyment, which they mistakenly fancy to be happiness; but can any mistake be more complete, or more fatal in its consequences? They are placed in this world, endowed with faculties which will enable them to promote the well-being of those about them, and by that means at the same time to promote their own; instead of which they neglect the opportunities God affords them for the right and beneficial employment of their talents, and insanely pervert them to the destruction of their health, their wealth, and their prospects, both in this world and the next. Who that has human feelings can look at this state of things, and not be led to ask himself, 'How will the people who live this way ever get to heaven?' or, might we not rather say, 'How are they to be kept out of hell?' and, recollect, even the vilest of these were once innocent children! Moreover, however humiliating it may be to admit the fact, as surely as God is our common Father, so surely are they our brethren and sisters? Can, then, anything be more self-evident than that it is both the interest and the duty of every one of us to do all in our power to prevent the young from swerving from the path of virtue?

The evil effects of this vicious and debasing practice do not obtrude themselves so much on public notice in the case of men as of women; but, without staying to inquire which of the two are the greatest sufferers, it is notorious that it is a dreadful scourge in both the army and navy, many thousands of men always being in hospital from the ravages it makes among them, a large portion of whom never are able to return to their duty: so large, indeed, is the number of victims as greatly to diminish the efficiency of our forces, and at the same time to inflict a heavy and wasteful expenditure on the country. This state of things, be it observed, implies a corresponding number of abandoned and infected women.

When a young man, instead of retiring at a proper time to his own chamber, spends his evening in revelry, and then shares the bed of a harlot, although he may manage to be at his post in the morning, and his daily associates be none the wiser, he knows that he has been guilty of conduct which is truly disgraceful, and of which he will be heartily ashamed that is, provided he has not lost all sense of right and wrong. He has, in fact, degraded himself to the level of his paramour, for whom, too, he cannot have an atom of respect; and without respect there cannot be any love that is worthy of the name.

But, besides the injury the fornicator does to himself, that which he inflicts on the woman is not to be overlooked or forgotten. If she were a maiden whom he seduced, the injury is little, if any, less than that of taking her life. If she had previously fallen, he helps to confirm her in her vicious course, and renders her reformation and consequent return to respectable society, and also her ultimate salvation, much more difficult and far less probable.

And, if we look to his own case, what is it? The longer he follows a vicious course, the more it becomes a confirmed habit; and it would be as reasonable to expect that half a life spent in the study of languages only should qualify a man for a surgeon or an engineer, as that a life of unchastity should qualify him for heaven, into which nothing impure can enter.

It is a well-established fact, which cannot be too generally known, that parents transmit to their children propensities to good or evil, especially the latter; and they in their turn transmit them to their posterity. It is, then, highly probable, and often happens, that when parents have indulged in certain vicious practices, whatever they may be, their children will be strongly inclined to the same. The children, for instance, of a drunkard, a miser, a tyrant, &c., will be very likely to resemble their parents; and this holds true no less with a sensualist. Moreover, physical diseases, especially that which has been alluded to, are often transmitted to innocent offspring, even after the parents have believed themselves thoroughly cured. Many may, in this way, trace the origin of their diseases as well as of their vices to their ancestors.

These considerations cannot be too strongly impressed on the attention of the young who are beginning life. It is only of healthy parents that healthy children are born. If young people had a right estimate of the responsibility they were about to undertake when they marry, they would shrink with horror from the danger of contamination, and of permanent injury to their health, should they yield to unchaste practices. No action of our lives but carries with it important ay, eternal consequences; and therefore the evil effects resulting from fornication may be felt by generations yet unborn.

Many will, perhaps, say that fornication always existed and always will. I demur to both propositions, and maintain, on the contrary, that it did not exist at the beginning; for then God saw that all was good: and if God gives to one man the power to reform, repent, and be regenerated which no one will deny He will doubtless give it to any one and all who ask for it; for He is love, and He loves every one of His creatures infinitely. We may, therefore, confidently look forward to the gradual decrease and ultimate extinction of this grievous curse of our race.

If you, my young friend, have already fallen into this sin, rely upon it you may shake it off entirely, provided you are sufficiently courageous, and look for strength to the only Fountain of all strength. As there is joy in heaven over one sinner that repenteth, so there is every encouragement for us to fight the good fight; for, although those who are against us are many and powerful, those who are on our side are both more numerous and more powerful.

Many well-intentioned people would like to keep the young ignorant of these sad and repulsive matters; so would I, if it were possible: but it is not; and I will not, therefore, pretend that I think you ignorant. Ignorance, be it remembered, is neither innocence nor security; and, on the other hand, knowledge does not involve either danger or guilt, but quite the contrary. I would then much rather help you to see this rampant vice in all its hideous deformity than attempt to conceal it from your notice.

"A little learning," it has been well said, "is a dangerous thing;" and, in like manner, a little knowledge respecting the relation between the sexes especially when that knowledge has been acquired in a disorderly way will be found to be highly dangerous; since the more valuable anything is, it is, on that very account, the more liable to be greatly abused: and it is not too much to say, that the evils and miseries resulting from the inordinate love of money or of wine howsoever enormous and deplorable they may bear no comparison to those inflicted on humanity by the abuse of that intense love for the other sex which God has implanted in every human breast for the wisest, the most beneficent, and the holiest of purposes. It seems to me that to be one of the most important duties of parents to give their children clear and definite notions on these matters much earlier than is usual. Too often the young get their minds poisoned with unchaste ideas, by ignorant or ill-disposed servants, schoolfellows, and others, long before the parents think the time has arrived when it will be prudent to initiate them into such subjects.

Rely upon it, fornication in its natural consequences, is intimately connected with misery and hell, to which, indeed, it directly leads; while, on the contrary, marriage as naturally and directly tends to happiness and heaven. Hence it behooves those parents who would wish to prevent their children from practicing this sin to do their utmost to put them in a position, as early as may be, to enter upon matrimony. If they do not, and their children fall into temptation, a heavy responsibility lies at their door. By waiting, in the hope of securing the respectability so much sought after, there is great danger of their falling into 'deadly SIN.'

Perhaps you will say, 'Marriage is all very well for those who can marry, but you cannot.' I ask, Why not? 'Because, in truth, you cannot afford it; at least your friends say so.' Now, although I have a strong objection to young persons marrying before their minds or their bodies are fully developed, still I do advocate early marriages; and I feel certain that not one tenth part so much mischief arises from them as from entering on a course of harlotry from which, alas! too many never emerge.

Dr. James Hodson makes the following strong and pertinent remarks:

"Nothing can possibly prove so certain a preservative [from vicious habits and the consequent diseases] as early and honorable MARRIAGE, formed upon a real and sincere affection. The arguments of prudence and youth, generally made use of against early marriages, are fallacious delusions, invented by the grand enemy of mankind: for Nature, both within and without, tells them they are not too young; and all the miseries that ever occurred from an early and a proper marriage are not in comparison to the ten-thousandth part of those evils which a vicious course of life, from fourteen to twenty-one, entails upon mankind! In the one instance, a few difficulties in life only are the greatest consequence, which love and mutual affection generally overcome; but in the other . . . It is the command of Heaven to marry, increase, and multiply: it is the suggestion of hell to forbid marriage, and to stir up unnatural affections in young people."

Burns who well knew what was right in his "Epistle to a Young Friend," says:

The sacred love of weel-placed love,
Luxuriantly indulge it;

57

But never tempt th' illicit rove,
Tho'naething should divulge it.

I waive the zuaetum of the sin;
The hazard of concealing;
But oh! It hardens a' within.
And petrifies the feeling.

Your friends, and you too, very probably, would wish you to settle respectably in something like the style to which you have been accustomed at home; and therefore, forsooth, you are to wait, no one knows how long. But if you look back only a generation or two, you will very probably find that some of your ancestors began life in a very humble fashion. Now it is by no means certain that they were less happy then than when they afterwards occupied a much higher position; and I maintain that happiness is what is most desirable, also that it is inseparable from virtue, and that it is not nearly so difficult of attainment as many imagine.

"Death is the gate of life." When, therefore, we leave this world our more real life first begins. And, without doubt, it is for this end that we are placed here, in a preparatory state, where we have ample opportunity of acquiring heavenly habits. Now, mark and see for yourself among your acquaintance whether it is not the most orderly, married people with families, those who are in the habitual endeavor to fulfill God's holy laws that are in the enjoyment of the greatest amount of real happiness. I by no means assert that they are so riotously joyous as the dissolute. The joys of the latter are merely transient, and soon give place to sorrow and remorse, or lead them on to ruin; while the joys of the former, partaking of the nature of Him from whom they spring, will doubtless go on increasing to eternity.

But I must come to a pause; the few pages to which I have limited myself will not permit me to do anything like full justice to my subject. I trust, however, that I have said enough to put some young persons who may be lead to read these remarks so far on their guard as to prevent them from entering a path which to all is dangerous, to very many fatal. In reference to all the numerous phases of this evil it may, with the greatest emphasis, be declared that "Prevention is better than cure."

CHAPTER X
A Special Chapter for Young Women.

Advice upon this subject is very much needed. I am assured that it is a subject not often talked of in families at least as it ought to be; nor is it much alluded to in the pulpit; and the result is that young people commonly get their notions about it from those only a little older than temselves, and who therefore know but little more than they do; or from those who form their opinions from the abuse they see of it, and so hold degrading and unworthy ideas respecting it. Sometimes all that is known about it amounts to this that it is a delightful thing to be married.

It is quite true that it often is, and always ought to be, delightful; still, you know, it is frequently quite the reverse. You cannot then be too cautious in the matter.

Nothing can be more orderly, right, proper, and holy than marriage. It is not, however, quite so simple an affair as you may fancy. Every good thing, and this is one of the best, requires some effort to obtain it; and unless you take the right course you must not expect to succeed.

You may often see a young woman who, from not entertaining correct views on the point, is certainly taking a wrong course; her endeavors being rather to make what she considers a good match, than, by acquiring kind and orderly habits, to qualify herself to become worthy of a worthy husband.

That the best things are liable to the greatest abuses is notorious; and from the lamentable fact that marriage is often abused, we may fairly infer its pre-eminent worth. In truth there is nothing more valuable. It is then highly injurious to entertain low notions respecting it; and men who indulge in loose conversation on the subject are likely, at the same time to think meanly of women. Beware of them; and if you hear them expressing such opinions in your presence, withdraw from them at once as unworthy of your company. Never fear but they will respect you the more for the rebuke.

Of course, you are looking forward to settle happily, and will do your best for that purpose. On this let me remark that all happiness that is, all that is genuine, and therefore worth of the name comes from connection with the One great source of all good; and He has freely and fully provided all the means necessary for our being happy, both here and hereafter. He has placed each of us where it is best for us to be, and in the circumstances that are best for us at the time; and this applies to you and to me now. How much soever appearances may be to the contrary, He cares as much for each of us as if we were the sole objects of His care. It is only by doing our duty, in humble dependence on His assistance, which He never withholds, that we can be happy. It behooves you then to consider well what is your duty, in order that you may do it, and may enjoy the blessings He is so ready to bestow. I hope you have been a loving and dutiful daughter, an affectionate sister and a faithful friend: then you may have good ground of hope for the future.

When a prospect of marriage occurs, you cannot do better than consult your mother, aunt, or other discreet relative that has your welfare at heart, from whom you may reasonably expect the best and most disinterested advice; and this it will be well for you to be guided by. Women of mature years can judge far better than you whether a man is likely to make a good husband. You should likewise quietly and cautiously make your own observations among your married acquaintance, especially where you believe there is a comfortable and happy home. You will doubtless find that, to a very great extent, this happy home depends on the wife's management and economy. Very often it happens that, where two husbands have the same income, with the same number of children, there will be comfort in the one home and discomfort in the other. Now there must be a reason for this; and you should endeavor to find it out, and profit by the lesson. It is said, 'Cleanliness is next to godliness;' and truly the value of cleanliness cannot be overrated. In point of time it should go before godliness; for where there is not cleanliness there can hardly be godliness; and the health of body and mind are greatly dependent on these two. Moreover, where can there be complete happiness without health?

One of the most prolific sources of matrimonial difficulties is the lack of knowledge on the part of wives of the duties of housekeeping. In these days there are a hundred young ladies who can drum on the piano to one who can make a good loaf of bread. Yet a hungry husband cares more for a good dinner than he does as long as his appetite is unappeased to listen to the music of the spheres. Heavy bread has made many heavy hearts, given rise to horrid dyspepsia and its herd of accompanying torments. Girls who desire that their husbands should be amiable and kind, should learn how to make good bread. When a young man is courting, he can live well at home; or, if he has to go a distance to pay his address, he usually obtains good meals at a hotel or an eating house; but when he is married and gets to housekeeping, his wife assumes the functions of his mother or his landlord, and it is fortunate for her if she has been educated so as to know what a good table is. Those who are entirely dependent on hired cooks make a very poor show at housekeeping. The stomach performs a very important part in the economy of humanity, and wives who are forgetful of this fact commit a serious mistake.

You know full well that most young men and most young women too are desirous of marrying and having a family; but they do not sufficiently consider that it is God who gives them this desire, and that for the wisest of purposes; not only that this world may be peopled, but also that its inhabitants may be prepared for heaven.

Nothing is more certain than that marriage affords the fairest opportunities for preparing for a better world. In it we have others dearer than ourselves to think about and provide for; and in doing so, we have often to practice that very useful virtue self-denial. Let me here impress upon you most deeply, that it is only by making others happy that we can become happy ourselves. The angels, we may be assured, are happy, because they are always actively good; and for a similar reason it is that God Himself is infinitely happy. If you try to secure your own happiness by any other means than a faithful discharge of your duty to God and your neighbor, you will certainly and deservedly fail.

I dare say you find that young men are fond of your

company and of paying you every polite attention, and you, as a right-minded woman, are well pleased to be so treated. It is due to you as a woman. Now each of them is or ought to be looking out for a wife; and it is well that you should know this. It is, too, more important than you perhaps are aware, that you should be carefully making your own observation, so that, when the time arrives for one of them to ask you to become his wife, you may not be taken by surprise, but may know how to act on the occasion.

Let me here caution you against a failing that is common among young women; I mean that of making themselves too cheap. They feel flattered by the attentions paid to them, and are not sufficiently aware that many young men are fond of indulging in flattery; and such, if they find a young woman weak enough to be pleased with it, will perhaps play upon her feelings and gain her affections, without having any honorable intentions towards her.

As a protection against such, I recommend you to have a proper respect for yourself, and to consider with what object or purpose you receive their attentions. If you respond without an object, you may be doing them wrong; if you accept them when they may have no right intentions, you allow them to wrong you. For this purpose consider well that you are a human being intended for an eternity of bliss. God has made you a WOMAN; and, believe me, there is no fairer, so there is no nobler creature than woman. She is formed to be her husband's help-mate and the mother of his children; and the all-important work of training these for heaven depends mainly upon her. Great, then, is her responsibility; but God has given her the requisite love and power to do her duty with satisfaction and delight. He has placed you in this beautiful world that by doing your duty as daughter, sister, wife, mother and friend, you may become fitted to enter His heavenly kingdom.

During your courtship let me entreat you to be very careful and circumspect. There is no period in life that can compare with this delightful season. It is or should be, full of sunshine and sparkling with the poetry of life; bur alas! to many it is the opposite. A want of judgment a momentary indiscretion, has not only blotted out this beautiful spring-time of life, but has marred, darkened and blighted the whole of the after life time.

No maiden can, under any circumstance, place her character in the hands of any man before marriage. No matter how sincere the love, how ardent the protestations, how earnest or plausible the pleadings, you must not, you can not surrender your honor. You must preserve your prudence and virtue, it is only by the possession of these, that you can keep the love and respect of your lover. Be firm, be circumspect, a rash word or a false step may extinguish forever all your bright hopes and prospective joys. Even should your lover redeem his promises and take you to be his wife, this indiscretion or crime will surely hang over you like a curse, creating discord, trouble and sorrow, the greatest portion of which will fall to your share.

You must know that young men, however amiable, worthy or honorable they may be, may in a moment of intense excitement, commit a sin, that in their calmer moments they would not be guilty of for worlds.

But under all circumstances, you will be looked upon to resist any advances and maintain your purity and virtue. No matter how high the tide of passion may run in unguarded moments and set in against heaven and against society, the terrible and painful ebb will surely follow and leave you stranded forever on the bleak and barren shore of your earthly existence.

There is no state of life more honorable, useful and happy, than that of a wife and mother. There must and ever will be inequalities of station, but happiness is equally attainable in them all. To be happy, however, you must be good; of course, I do no mean absolutely good; for "there is none good but One;" but I mean that you should be relatively good, and should aim at becoming better and more innocent as you advance in life. Now you cannot respect yourself unless you know that you are worthy of respect; and if you do not respect yourself, you cannot expect that anybody else will; and in such case you will not be worthy of the love of a good man, and none such will be likely to pay court to you. If, however, you take the right means, in which I include prayer for divine guidance, you will have the respect and friendship of all your acquaintance; and then in God's own time and, let me add, without your seeking it, the man whom you can make happy, and who can make you happy, will present himself and propose to make you his wife, if it be God's will that you should become one.

Here are two very important points for your consideration; first that it should be your constant endeavor to make your husband happy; and, second, that, before you consent to marry him, you should ascertain that he has those qualifications that will secure your happiness. It most nearly concerns yourself that you do your duty to God and your neighbor at all times, so that it becomes your habit: and you will find it much easier, and safer too, to do it every day rather than only on particular occasions; for this would require a special effort, and for the time, perhaps, put you into a state of excitement, which, in all probability, would be succeeded by a depression of spirits. What you should rather aim at is a uniformly cheerful state of mind resulting from a conscious and confident dependence on Providence. If your husband knows from experience that such is your character he cannot fail, provided he be worthy of you, to be content and happy.

It is the nature of young women to be affectionate, and it is pleasant and usual for them to have several friends enjoying more or less of their confidence. Among these may be included some of their male acquaintance. Now, while they may esteem each of these as they would a dear cousin, they should know and act upon the knowledge, that it is only to one they can give their unlimited confidence and undivided affection as a wife. It is the height of cruelty and wickedness for either a man or a woman to trifle with another's affection. Such base conduct has cost many a young woman her health and peace, and even her life, and cannot therefore be too much deprecated and avoided.

Let me then advise you to be very cautious before you allow a young man to pay you such marked attentions as may lead to marriage. It is not, you know, to terminate in seven years, like an apprenticeship or a commercial partnership, but it is an engagement for the life of one of the parties. I want you then to profit by the experience of others, too many of whom enter into marriage from light and low considerations; and not to settle in life till you, and also your friends, see that there is a reasonable prospect of your securing happiness, as well as comfort and a respectable position.

When a young woman has property, or expects it, or is possessed of superior personal attractions, she should be especially prudent in her conduct towards the numerous admirers which such qualifications usually attract. No woman should allow herself to accept the attentions of any man who does not possess those sterling qualities which will command her respect, or whose love is directed to her fortune or beauty rather than herself. On such a one she can place no reliance; for, should illness or misfortune overtake her, she may find herself deprived of that love which she had valued as the great treasure of her life. Possessed of this, she feels that earthly riches are but of secondary importance, and that the want of them can never make her poor.

Moreover, a worthier man than any of her interested suitors, may have a sincere respect and affection for her, but be kept in the background by the over-zealous attention of his rivals. Still, if she has sufficient self-command to patiently and calmly investigate their general private character, she may find reason to decline their suit, and may discover that the more modest and retiring youth is the one that is deserving of her love.

While on this subject, let me caution you against the foolish affectation some girls practice in order to attract the attention of young men. In their company, be natural in your manners, open and friendly and ready to converse on general subjects; not appearing to expect that every one who pays you the ordinary courtesies of society is going to fall in love with you. This mode of behavior, which is more common with those who are vain of their beauty than with others, frequently leads to such young women being more neglected than their less pretending sister; for prudent young men, who are impressed with the necessity of a right decision in the all important step of marriage, instinctively shrink from those who seem unwilling to give them a fair opportunity of judging whether their hearts and minds are as attractive as their persons.

You may innocently admire many a young man for the noble qualitites God has bestowed upon him, without at all entertaining the idea either that he would make you happy as his wife, or you him as your husband. Thank God, we are constituted of such different temperaments that all may find suitable partners without clashing with others' tastes, if they will only be content to watch and wait.

It is the part of a young man to watch, to be actively desirous of meeting with a suitable partner. In doing this his first consideration should be to seek for such a one as he can make happy, not to look primarily for beauty, fortune, wit, or accomplishments, things all very good in themselves, but by no means constituting the essentials of happiness. If he is influenced by pure and simple motives, he will not find or expect to find, more than one that can satisfy his desire; and he will not be in much danger of exciting the envy or the rivalry of his companions.

On the other hand, it is becoming in a young woman to wait patiently, till, from the assiduous and respectful attentions of a young man, she can have no doubt that he is in earnest; when, and not before, she may freely give him her company, and with every expectation of a happy result. Be assured that no sensible young man is ever attracted by a young woman whom he sees on the lookout for a lover; he is more likely to think meanly of her, and to avoid her society.

It may, however, happen that a young man makes the offer before the young woman knows enough of him for it to be right for her to accept it, and before he on his part ought to take the step. In such a case it would be well for her, even supposing she is inclined to like him, to tell him that he has taken her by surprise, and that she cannot think of entering on so important a subject without consulting her friends, to whom she accordingly refers him. It would then become her duty to intimate to him that, although his attentions are agreeable to them, he must wait a while, till, from further acquaintance, they are enabled to judge whether it will conduce to the mutual happiness of their daughter and himself for her to accept the offer he has so kindly made.

But it is not only young men who are apt to be hasty in these matters: it is, as is well known, not uncommon for parents, especially mothers, very soon after a young man has begun to pay attention to their daughter, to give him to understand that they wish to know his intentions with reference to her. By such proceedings a young man may be taken aback, and either hurry into a match which turns out unhappily, or be led to withdraw from a union which might have resulted in the happiness of all the parties concerned.

That your parents should wish you to be married, is only natural, especially if their own marriage has been a happy one. It will be gratifying to them to see a worthy young man paying attention to you, and, most probably, they will let things take their own course. Marriage is too important a matter to admit of being hastened.

There are, I am aware, unwise parents who, from various motives, will throw obstacles in the way of young people who are desirous of coming together. Some are so selfish as to be unwilling to part with their daughter, preferring their own happiness to hers. Others are so silly as to think no ordinary man good enough for her, and therefore, if they had their own way, would leave her to become an old maid. Fortunately, such short-sighted people are not unfrequently outwitted.

If your parents are as I hope reasonable in their views and expectations, one of the chief concerns of their life will be the promotion of your happiness; and it behooves you to pay the utmost deference to their opinion; and should they, from circumstances they become aware of, deem it advisable that you should either postpone or even break off an engagement, they will, doubtless, give you such weighty reasons as will justify you in acting on their advice. Where, however, as sometimes happens, they unwisely refuse their consent to their child's marriage, at a time when she well knows, from her own feeling, and also from the sanction she receives from the opinion of trustworthy and judicious friends, that she would be making a real sacrifice were she to comply with their wishes, if, I say, under such circumstances, she acts disobediently and marries the man she loves, more blame attaches to the parents than to herself; and the sooner they forgive her the better.

It is very common for young men, when going into the company of young women, together with their best dress to put on their best behavior: in fact, to assume a character which is not their natural one, but far superior to it. Some hold the opinion that "All is fair in love and war." To me it appears there cannot be greater folly and wickedness than for young people who are thinking of marriage to attempt to deceive each other. What is the good of it? A very short period of married life will entirely dispel the illusion. I suppose people of the world may think it fair to overreach one another in their dealings, saying, "Everyone for himself." They have no intention of seeking to promote the other's happiness: present gain is all they want. But a married pair, to be happy, must respect and esteem, as well as love, each other; and this cannot be attained except by the constant endeavor to be as well as to appear true and good.

That young men should behave well in the presence of women is only natural and right. None but a fool would do otherwise. But you, long before thinking of marrying, should take all fair means to learn what are the general conduct and habits of your male acquaintance, in their family circle and with their daily connection. Are they good-humored and kind, able to bear the troubles they meet with? Are they industrious, frugal, temperate, religious, chaste? Have they had the prudence to insure against sickness and death? Or, on the other hand, are they addicted to drinking, smoking, betting, keeping late hours, frequenting casinos, &c.? Your mother and other prudent friends will assist you to find this out. Those who do not come up to the proper standard, however agreeable they may be as acquaintance, certainly cannot make good husbands. In company of such, it behooves you to be well on your guard, and accept no attention from them. Should you marry such a one, you would be sure to be miserable.

While, however, it is quite right that you should be careful about the character of the young man who is paying court to you, it is of far more importance to you that you should be careful about your own, and this whether you marry or not. Indeed, a chief object in our being placed in this world is that we may acquire good habits, and so be fitted to associate with "the Just made perfect in heaven."

Be very guarded in your actions and demeanor. Cultivate purity of heart and thought. No woman is fit to become a wife who is not perfectly modest in word, deed and thought. No young man, who is worth having, would ever entertain the thought for a moment of taking the girl for a wife who is habitually careless in her conversation and displays a levity in her manners. Young men may like free and hearty girls to laugh and talk with, but as to taking one for a wife, let me assure you they would not tolerate the idea for a moment.

You may at times be unavoidably compelled to hear a vulgar word spoken, or an indelicate illusion made: in every instance maintain a rigid insensibility. It is not enough that you cast down your eyes and turn your head, you must act as if you did not hear it; appear as if you did not comprehend it. You ought to receive no more impression from remarks or allusions of this character than a block of wood. Unless you maintain this standing, and preserve this high-toned purity of manner, you will be greatly depreciated in the opinion of all men whose opinion is worth having, and you deprive yourself of much influence and respect which it is your privilege to possess and exert.

Courtship, after all, is a momentous matter. After taking all the counsel that may be offered, you must at last, in a great measure, rely on your own judgment. Within a few short months you have to decide, from what you can see of a man, whether you will have him, in preference to your parents, friends, and all others that you know, to be a life companion. What can you do? How shall you judge? How arrive at a correct conclusion? My dear young girl, there is only One to assist you. He in His mercy to your helplessness and weakness, has given to every virtuous and pure-minded woman a wonderful, mysterious and subtle instinct; a peculiar faculty that cannot be analyzed by reason, a faculty that men do not possess, and one in which they do not generally believe. At this all important period, this eventful crisis in your life, this womanly instinct guides and saves you. You can feel in a moment the presence or influence of a base, sensual and unworthy nature. An electric-like thrill animates you, and you are naturally repulsed from him. When your suitor is a man of incongruous temper, ungenial habits, and of a morose and unsympathetic disposition, this same precious, divine instinct acts, and the man feels, though he cannot tell why, that all his arts and aspirations are in vain; it will seldom be necessary for you to tell him verbally of his failure; but should such a one blindly insist upon intruding his attentions, do not hesitate to tell him kindly but firmly your decision. Should your suitor be one who is worthy, who will make you happy, this same blessed instinct will whisper in your soul the happy news. From the first interview there is frequently thrown around the maiden a peculiar, undefined spell; she will feel differently in his presence, and watch him with other eyes than she has for the rest of men, and in due time, when he shall ask her to decide upon the question which shall seal the temporal and eternal destiny of two human souls, she will gladly respond, giving in loving trustfulness that which is the most precious, the most enviable thing on earth: a maiden's heart, a woman's love.

Many persons of both sexes, however amiable and pure their minds may be, should conscientiously abstain from marriage. This applies to all who have a tendency to consumption, scrofula, insanity or any other of those diseases which are so frequently transmitted to offspring. This very important matter is not sufficiently known, and therefore is not attended to as it ought to be; hence the great amount of sickness and early death among children.

The tendency to inherit qualities is very evident in the case of drunkards, whose children are often inclined to practice the vice of their parents. The children of the blind and of the deaf and dumb are also liable to be afflicted as their parents were. These facts go far to show that it is literally true that the sins of the fathers are visited upon the children. It is, however, gratifying to know and there are many well-attested cases to prove it that, whereas the children born to a man while he was addicted to drunkenness were similarly addicted to that vice, those born after he gave up his vicious indulgence, and by that means improved his bodily health, were free from the evil tendency.

One strong reason why near relations should not inter-marry is that, as the same general tendencies prevail in families, when the parents are nearly related, they are very likely to have the same evil tendency, whatever that may be; and, therefore, there is a great probability that their children will also have the same, but more strongly developed; and, consequently, the difficulty of their overcoming it will be much increased.

How plainly then is it the duty of those about to marry, as well as of those who are married, to strive to their utmost, with God's help, to overcome disorderly habits of every kind; for, be assured, it is only by such means they can hope to be blessed with good and healthy children, and thereby contribute to their own happiness, and at the same time to the improvement of the race as subject both of this world and of heaven.

As it is by no means certain that you will marry, and the time may come when it will no longer be convenient to your parents to support you, it will be good for you, keeping these contingencies in mind, to qualify yourself to earn your own maintenance by some honest industry. You will then have a right feeling of independence, and will not be tempted to marry, as too many young women do, not from the true principle of sincere affection, but mainly for a living. They may thus obtain a com-petency, and jog on comfortably; but they have no right to expect that genuine happiness which I recommend you to aim at. When, too, you see so many left widows, with small families, and, as we say, totally unprovided for, you will become sensible of the soundness of the advice I am offering you. As the Lord's tender mercies are over all His works, it is evident, from what is occur-ring around us, that trouble and adversity are better suited to the state of some people, to prepare them for their eternal destina-tion, than any amount of prosperity would be. The poor are no less His children than the rich, and He cares equally, that is, infinitely, for them all. It is certainly wise, then, to be prepared to meet adversity, should He suffer it to come upon you.

Again, suppose you should not have any suitable offer of marriage, such as you would feel it your duty to accept, you are not on that account to be disheartened, and fancy yourself overlooked by Providence. Single life is evidently the best for some persons: they escape many troubles which perhaps they would find hard to bear. There are many ways in which single people can lead a useful life, and be as happy as the day is long. No one that is actively useful can be unhappy. What do you see around you? Many, I admit, who are not so happy as we should like them to be; but in most cases, if we could fully investigate the matter, it would perhaps be found to have arisen from their thinking too much about themselves and not enough for others. But, on the other hand, it not unfrequently happens, when a woman is left, and sees that the support and welfare of herself and her children depend on her own exertions, she is enabled successfully to put forth her energies, and to employ her talents which, till she needed them, she hardly knew she possessed, as to surprise herself and the most sanguine of her friends.

Now, it must be confessed that we are fallen creatures, and therefore prone to evil. We are consequently always in danger of going wrong and forming bad habits; but our heavenly Father watches over us at all times, and gives us power "to refuse the evil and choose the good." We are, I know full well, too much inclined to yield to evil influences; still, as we always have divine aid if we implore it, I am not sure that, on the whole, it is not as easy to acquire good habits as bad ones. This much is certain, that whichever we acquire, good or bad, they are likely to remain with us, and are not easily to be got rid of.

Among the subjects deserving attention, as affecting our happiness, is one on which perhaps I am not entitled to say much. I refer to dress. Now, I hold it to be a duty for people to dress well, that is, according to their position, means, and age; and this not so much for their own sakes as for the sake of giving pleasure to others. It is, I admit, difficult to determine how much of one's income should be devoted to dress; but I think few will deny that, at present, dress occupies too much time, attention and money. For my own part, I confess, I am most affected by female dress; and although certainly I like to see women well dressed, and would rather see them a little too fine than slovenly, I am often pained at witnessing the extravagance and, to me, ridiculous taste exhibited. Whenever I see a handsome and expensive dress trailing in the dirt, I regard it as culpable waste and in bad taste; and when I see it accidentally trodden on, I am not sorry. I am inclined to believe that many women can hardly find time or opportunity to perform any useful duty: they have quite as much as they, poor things, can do, to take care of their dress. I also believe and this is the serious point of the matter that many a young man is deterred from soliciting a maiden in marriage, by knowing that his means would not enable him to let her dress as he is accustomed to see her; and this is doubtless one of the many reasons why so many of both sexes remain unmarried. I hold, too, that whatever forms an obstacle to marriage has a tendency, at the same time, to obstruct the entrance to heaven.

I will now allude to some of the duties which will devolve upon you as a wife; and recollect that it is only the faithful discharge of these duties that your happiness, here and hereafter, mainly depends. All labor is honorable, and you know who it is that says, "My Father worketh hitherto, and I work." Being married, you must make your husband feel, "There is no place like home." His business will probably take him from home most of the day, and it should be your care as I doubt not it will be your delight to see to his comfort, both before he starts and when he returns. It may sometimes happen, in his fighting the battle of life, that he has to encounter much that is unpleasant, and he may return home depressed. You will then have to cheer him; and be assured, no one can do it so effectually, so pleasantly, aye, and so easily, as yourself.

It is not to sweep the house and make the bed, and darn the socks, and cook the meals, chiefly, that a man wants a wife. If this is all he needs, hired help can do it cheaper than a wife. If this is all, when a young man calls to see a young lady, send him into the pantry to taste the bread and cake she has made. Send him to inspect the needle-work and bed-making; or put a broom into her hands and send him to witness its use. Such things are important and the wise young man will quietly look after them. But what a true man most wants of a true wife is her companionship, sympathy, courage, and love. The way of life has many dreary places in it, and a man needs a companion to go with him. A man is sometimes overtaken with misfortune; he needs one to stand by and sympathize. He has some stern battles to fight with poverty, with enemies, and with sin; and he needs a woman who , while he puts his arm around her, he feels that he has something to fight for, and she will help him fight; that will put her lips to his ear and whisper words of counsel, and her hands to his heart and impart new inspirations. All through life through storm and through sunshine, conflict and victory, and through adverse and favoring winds man needs woman's love. The heart yearns for it. A sister's or a mother's love will hardly supply the need. Yet many seek for nothing further than success in housework. Justly enough, half of these get nothing more; the other half, surprised beyond measure, have got more than they sought. Their wives surprise them by bringing a nobler idea of marriage, and disclosing a treasury of courage, sympathy and love.

And I would here caution you against giving way to little misunderstandings in early married life. Sometimes trifling matters for want of some forbearance or concession on one side or the other, perhaps on both sides, accumulate into serious results. These differences might be avoided by married partners studying each other's peculiarities of character, with the aim of mutually correcting, in a kindly spirit, any wrong tendency or temper which may sometimes show itself. Should you find you have inadvertently given pain or uneasiness to your husband, do not rest until you have ascertained the cause of his disquiet, and succeed in allaying the unhappy feeling. The earnest desire to please each other should by no means terminate on the wedding day, but as studiously continue through married life. Each should always endeavor to think the best of the other, and instantly reject every thought that might tend to weaken the bond of mutual preference and perfect trust.

If he be wise, he will leave the housekeeping entirely to you; his time and attention can be better employed elsewhere. To enable you to do this wisely, you should, long before you marry, become familiar with the quality and prices of articles of consumption, and where they can be best obtained. Every wife should be able to cook well, whether she had to do it herself or not. Health and good humor greatly depend upon the food's being of good quality, well cooked, and nicely served up. She should also be able, if needful, to make and mend her own and children's clothes.

Too much importance cannot be attached to cleanliness. Men may be careless as to their own personal appearance, and may, from the nature of their business, be negligent in their dress, but they dislike to see any disregard in the dress and appearance of their wives. Nothing so depresses a man and makes him dislike and neglect his home as to have a wife who is slovenly in her dress and unclean in her habits. Beauty of face and form will not compensate for these defects; the charm of purity and cleanliness never ends but with life itself. These are matters that do not involve any great labor or expense. the use of the bath, and the simplest fabrics, shaped by your own supple fingers, will be all that is necessary. These attractions will act like a magnet upon your husband. Never fear that there will be any influence strong enough to take him from your side.

An experience of many years of observation has convinced me that where a pure, industrious and cheerful wife meets her husband with a bright smile on the threshold of her dwelling, that man will never leave her home for any other place.

As all people are liable to illness, every young woman should aim at being an efficient nurse. In case of illness, it is now generally admitted that good nursing is of more value than medicine. To a sick husband, a little gruel or other trifle prepared and given by wife's own hand will confer much more benefit than if prepared and given by another. Should it happen to you to fall ill, you may expect your husband will do his best; but you must not be surprised if he is not your equal in that department. Nursing is one of the many useful things which women do better than men. A practical knowledge of nursing will enable you to be useful beyond your own family, and will enhance your value as a neighbor.

You have often, I trust, experienced the pleasure of serving others from disinterested motives, and found that the pleasure has been deeper and purer when you have engaged in doing good to those who could not make you any return. This you have found to be the case whenever you have had charge of a baby, one of those little ones of whom the Lord says: "Their angles do always behold the face of my Father who is in Heaven." You have perhaps been surprised to find how easy it was to perform such a duty; and let me assure you that you may always expect to find it easy to perform your duty in that state of life to which it shall please God to call you. He never requires anything from any of his creatures beyond what He gives them power to do. He is no hard task-master. You have only to look to Him, and do your best, and then you may safely leave the result in His hands. Our Lord says, "My yoke is easy, and my burden is light."

Of all God's creatures, I know no happier one than a young mother with a good husband and a healthy baby. I say a healthy baby, for that implies healthy parents, especially a healthy mother. She may justly feel proud that God has intrusted a young immortal to her care, and she should at all times bear in mind that it is His gift. While it is on all hands considered honorable to hold a commission for the President and to fill a high office, contributing to the welfare of many people, a mother may feel her office, at least as honorable, seeing she has entrusted to her the rearing and training of an immortal being, and that she holds her commission direct from the King of kings. For, recollect, it is only by God's blessing that she becomes a mother; for such is the present state of society that many very worthy married people have not the privilege of offspring, although they are intensely fond of children, and seem to have no other earthly want. They may nevertheless be very useful and therefore, happy in a different sphere, by the adoption of nephews and nieces, or in some similar way.

At the birth of her first child, there is opened in the mother's heart a new well of love, such as she had not known before; and although she may fancy that this is all spent upon her babe, it is not so; for she loves her God, her husband, and everybody else better than ever. The father too, is similarly affected: he also has a warmer love for his wife and for all his connections.

A similar idea is well expressed by Moehler, a German writer, who says: "the power of selfishness, which is inwoven with our whole being, is altogether broken by marriage; and, by degrees, love, becoming more and more pure, takes its place. When a man marries, he gives himself up entirely to another being: in this affair of life he first goes out of himself, and inflicts the first deadly wound on his egotism. By every child with which his marriage is blessed, Nature renews the same attack on his self-hood; causes him to live less for himself, and more even without being distinctly conscious of it for others; his heart expands in proportion as the claimants upon it increase; and, bursting the bonds of its former narrow exclusiveness, it eventually extends its sympathy to all around."

Whenever a mother is supplying her baby with the food which God has so wisely provided for it, or is ministering to any other of its numerous and increasing wants, she may feel that everything she does for it is pleasing to her heavenly Father, and has its immediate reward in the delight she experiences in the act.

I can fancy that, when a mother has washed her baby, and before she dresses it, has a good romp with it, smothering it with kisses, calling it all the beauties and darlings and pets and jewels she can think of, and talking any amount of nonsense at the top of her voice, the baby all the while cooing, chirping, or even screaming with delight; at such a time, I say, I can easily fancy that the angels are looking on approvingly and enjoying the scene. And why not? "Of such is the Kingdom of Heaven."

From the time that an infant first becomes conscious of its wants, and long afterwards, it looks to its mother to supply them all, fully believing her able to do it. She is, in fact, in place of God to it: and it would be well for many of us if we trusted our heavenly Father as simply and as fully as the infant does its earthly mother.

Those who know no better, when they see a mother patiently watching her sleeping babe, might wonder that she does not feel the want of company. She has, however, company that they know not of, and of which even she herself may not be conscious. If only our eyes were open, we might see that she is not only one that is so engaged, that angels are also occupied in watching the babe and in supporting her. I entirely agree with Dr. Watts, when, in his "Cradle Hymn," he makes the mother say:

Hush, my babe, lie still and slumber.

Holy angels guard thy bed.

You probably know the beautiful Irish superstition that, when a baby smiles in its sleep, the angels are whispering to it.

Before I became a father, I took little or no interest in babies; I rather thought them troublesome things. But the arrival of one of my own wrought a great change in me. I enlarged at once my views and my heart, and I had higher and stronger motives to exertion. My interest in them has not yet begun to weaken; and I have no reason to think it ever will.

Girls are different from boys. God makes the intellect predominate in males, and affection in females. Accordingly, a little girl early shows a love for a doll, regarding it quite as her baby, and never taking into account that it is not alive. She has many of a mother's cares and anxieties, as well as pleasures about it, indeed as many as she is then capable of. It is a constant source of amusement and employment to her. In all this we may plainly see the hand of Providence: it forms a suitable introduction to some of the interesting and important duties which will devolve on her if it should be His good pleasure for her to become a mother.

The other day I met a group of four or five little girls, the principal one, some nine years old, very carefully carrying a baby. On my saying to her, "You seem almost as pleased as if it were your own baby," she gave me an innocent smile, and said rather proudly, I thought "It is my own, please sir." I took it she was the sister, and not a hired nurse.

You will, I dare say, readily see the object I now have in view. It is that I wish to impress on you how desirable it is that you should take every opportunity of becoming acquainted with the habits and wants of babies, and the best way of managing them. The more you have to do with them the more you will like the labor, and the easier and more delightful it will become. It is fair that, before you have children of your own, you should get your knowledge as to the management of them, by experience with other people's. I take it for granted you will at all times do your best for them. You will then have but little cause to fear accident; and if accident should happen as with all your care it sometime will you will have more confidence in your powers, and will be more likely to do what is best at the moment, than if you were unused to children. Much of the disease and early death that happens among children arises from the ignorance of the mothers; who, however, are much more to be pitied than blamed in the matter. They had never been properly taught their duties toward their future offspring.

It will be very advantageous to you, to procure a copy of a very valuable work called "Our Own Family Doctor."
[OUR OWN FAMILY DOCTOR AND COMPLETE MEDICAL ADVISER, containing every known fact that can promote health, cure disease or prolong life. Price $2. Hurst & Co., Publishers, New York.]

It contains a vast amount of valuable information respecting health, disease and other kindred subjects, written in so plain a style that simple people cannot fail to understand it. The volume I consider so suitable to young women about to marry, that parents should not hesitate to place it in their hands. I would especially mention the chapters entitled "Women and their Diseases," "Children and their Care," "Accidents and Emergencies," and the chapter to the youth of both sexes.

These portions of the work alone are worth tenfold more than the price asked for the whole work. I am certain they are calculated to save the lives of many children and not a few mothers.

Few mothers are, perhaps, sufficiently aware of the great influence which their manners, habits and conversation have upon the tender minds of their children, even from birth. The child should grow up with a feeling of reverence for its parents, which can only be the case when wisdom as well as affection is exercised in its bringing up. Hence the necessity of the mother's fitting herself, both intellectually and morally, for her sacred office, that the child may become accustomed to yield perfect obedience to her wishes from a principle of love, and may acquire, as it advances in life, the habit of yielding a like obedience to that which is right.

As you well know that you are not perfect yourself, you must be prepared to find that your husband has also his imperfections; and it is no unimportant part of your duty to help him to get rid of them. Indeed it is one of the highest uses of marriage for each partner to assist the other on the journey to the heavenly Canaan. But, before you attempt to point out a fault in him, consider how you had best proceed, so as to attain your object; for, unless you adopt a judicious mode, and an affectionate as well as an earnest manner, you may do as much harm as good. You must also carefully watch your opportunity; for what would be favorably received at one time, and under certain circumstances, might, under other circumstances, give offence, and altogether fail of the good effect intended and hoped for. You do not know how powerful you may be for good to your husband. There is much truth in the saying, "A man is what a woman makes him."

Respecting the good influence of virtuous love, Tennyson says:

For indeed I know
Of no more subtle master under heaven
Than is the maiden passion for a maid.
Not only to keep down the base in man,
But teach him thought and amiable words,
And courtliness, and the desire of fame,
And love of truth, and all that makes a man.

Previous to marriage, it will be expedient for you not to give your lover that full and unlimited confidence which it will be your duty and your inclination, too to give him when he becomes your husband. I refer chiefly to family and other private matters, not to anything he ought to know to enable him to judge of your character and position. Many unhappy marriages have been brought about through the young woman's letting it be known that she has "great expectations." A worthless fellow may, in consequence, have succeeded in winning her hand.

There is another point to which I must just allude before I close this address. It is doubtless the order of Providence for marriages to take place, when possible, on our arriving at the age of maturity. But I would guard you against the evil results of too early marriages, before either body or mind is perfectly matured. We scarcely need consult either medical or moral science to satisfy ourselves on this by no means trifling point.

We may find in society too many sad instances of such immature and indiscreet unions. The minds of young persons should be expanded by a certain amount of experience in the world before entering upon engagements involving so many momentous duties.

In your daily walks abroad, if you examine the countenances of those you meet, you will doubtless be led to conclude that there is a great deal of disease and misery in the world; but, judging from my own observation, I think you will find that the greater number of persons exhibit signs of health and happiness. Much of the disease and misery with which the world is afflicted, is the direct result of the misconduct of the individuals themselves; but no little of it attributable to their parents, who have neglected or violated God's law of health, their misconduct thus affecting their descendants "to the third and fourth generation." I cannot therefore, too much impress upon you the importance of your honestly trying to find out any bad habits to which you are inclined, with a view to getting rid of them, one by one, and supplying their place with good habits. By pursuing this course, you will not only do much for your own happiness, but also for that of your children, if God should bless you with a family. Children, you know, are often striking likenesses of their parents; and in their minds and habits, they likewise often resemble them. You should strive then to be good, not from mere self-love, and that you may get to heaven, but because your duty to others requires it.

Earl Granville, when laying the foundation stone of the Alexandria Orphanage, in England, thus expressed himself in reference to the great value of children:

"Few will deny that a child is 'an inestimable loan,' as it has been called, or refuse to acknowledge with one of our great poets, that 'the world would be somewhat of a melancholy one if there were no children to gladden it.' Children, more than any other earthly thing, equalize the conditions of society to rich and poor; they bring an interest, a pleasure, and an elevation, which nothing else that is earthly does."

Now young people, before they think of engaging themselves, should clearly know each other's peculiar views of religion; because if they differ seriously on this point, there is danger of its interfering with that full confidence which is so essential to happiness.

CHAPTER XI
Sexual Intercourse Its Laws and Conditions
Its Use and Abuse.

There is an increasing and alarming prevalence of nervous ailments, and complicated disorders, that could be traced to have their sole origin from this source. Hypochondria, in its various phases, results from the premature and unnatural waste of the seminal fluid. There speedily ensues a lack of natural heat, a deficiency of vital power, and consequently indigestion, melancholy, languor, and defection ensue, the victim becomes enervated and spiritless, loses the very attributes of man and premature old age soon follows.

It is a prevalent error, that it is necessary for the semen to be ejected at certain times from the body, and that its retention is incompatible with sound health and vigor of body and mind. This is a very fallacious idea. The seminal fluid is too precious, Nature bestows too much care in its elaboration, for it to be wasted in this unproductive manner. It is intended, when not used for the purpose of procreation, to be re-absorbed again into the system, giving vigor of body, strength and elasticity to the mind, making the individual strong, active and self-reliant. When kept as Nature intended, it is a perpetual fountain of life and energy, a vital force which acts in every direction, a motive power, which infuses manhood into every organ of the brain and every fibre of the body.

The law of sexual morality for childhood is one of utter negation of sex. Every child should be kept pure and free from amative excitement, and the least amative indulgence, which is unnatural and doubly hurtful. No language is strong enough to express the evils of amative excitement and unnatural indulgence before the age of puberty; and the dangers are so great that I see no way so safe as thorough instruction regarding them at the earliest age. A child may be taught, simply as a matter of science, as one learns botany, all that is needful to know, and such knowledge may protect it from the most terrible evils.

The law for childhood is perfect purity, which cannot be

too carefully guarded and protected by parents, teachers, and all caretakers. The law for youth is perfect continence a pure vestalate alike in both sexes. No indulgence is required by one more than the other, for both Nature has made the same provision. The natures of both are alike, and the least exercise of the amative function is an injury to one as to the other. Men expect that women shall come to them in marriage chaste and pure from the least defilement. Women have a right to expect the same of their husbands. Here the sexes are upon a perfect equality.

On the subject, Dr. Carpenter, in his physiological works, has written like a man of true science, and therefore of true morality. He lays it down as an axiom that the development of the individual, and the reproduction of the species, stand in an inverse ratio to each other. He says:

"The augmented development of the generative organs at puberty can only be rightly regarded as preparatory to the exercise of these organs. The development of the individual must be completed before the procreative power can properly be exercised for the continuance of the race." And in the following extract from his "Principles of Human Physiology," he confirms my statement respecting the unscientific and libertine advice of too many physicians: "The author would say to those of his younger readers, who urge the wants of nature as an excuse for the illicit gratification of the sexual passions, 'Try the effects of close mental application to some of those ennobling pursuits to which your profession introduces you, in combination with vigorous bodily exercise, before you assert that appetite is unrestrainable, and act upon that assertion.' Nothing tends so much to increase the desire as the continual direction of the mind toward the objects of its gratification, whilst nothing so effectually represses it as a determined exercise of the mental faculties upon other objects, and the expenditure of nervous energy in other channels. Some works which have issued from the medical press contain much that is calculated to excite, rather than to repress, the propensity; and the advice sometimes given by practitioners to their patients is immoral, as well as unscientific."

Every man and every woman, living simply, purely, and temperately respecting the laws of health in regard to air, food, dress, exercise, and habits of life, not only can live in the continence of a pure virgin life when single, and in the chastity which should be observed by all married partners but be stronger, happier, every way better by so living.

Chastity is the conservation of life and the consecration of the forces to the highest use. Sensuality is the waste of life and the degradation of its forces to pleasure divorced from use. Chastity is life, sensuality is death.

From the age of puberty to marriage the law is the same for both sexes. Full employment of mind and body, temperance, purity, and perfect chastity in thought, word, and deed. The law is one of perfect equality. There is no license for the male which is not equally the right of the female. There is no physiological ground for any indulgence in one case more than in the other. No man has any more right to require or expect purity in the woman who is to be his wife, than the woman has to require and expect purity in her husband. It is a simple matter of justice and right. No man can enter upon an amative relation with a woman except in marriage, without manifest injustice to his future wife, unless he allow her the same liberty; and also without a great wrong to the woman, and to her possible husband.

It is contended that the sins of men against chastity are more venal than those of women, because of the liability of women to have children. But men are also liable to be the fathers of children, who are deeply wronged by the absence of paternal care. The child has its rights, and every child has the right to be born in homes, respectable wedlock, of parents able to give it a sound constitution and the nurture and education it requires. The child who lacks these conditions is grievously wronged by both father and mother.

The law of marriage is that the mature man and woman, with sound health, pure lives, and a reasonable prospect of comfortably educating a family, when drawn to each other by the attraction of a mutual love, should chastely and temperately unite for offspring. The sexual relation has this chief and controlling purpose. The law of nature is intercourse for reproduction. Under the Christian law, marriage is the symbol of the union of Christ and the Church; husband and wife are one in the Lord; they are to live in married chastity, not in lust and uncleanness; and there cannot be a more hideous violation of Christian morals than for a husband to wreak his sensuality upon a feeble wife against her wishes, when she has no desire for offspring, and no power to give them the healthy constitutions and maternal care which is their right.

The law of Christian morality is very clear. It is the sexual union first and chiefly for its principal object. It is for the husband to refrain from it whenever it is not desired; whenever it would be hurtful to either; whenever it would be a waste of life; whenever it would injure mother or child, as during pregnancy and lactation. A man who truly loves a woman, must respect and reverence her, and cannot make her the victim of his inordinate and unbridled, selfish and sensual nature. He will be ever, from the first moment of joyful possession, to the last of his life, tender, delicate, considerate, deferent, yielding to her slightest wishes in the domain of love, and never encroaching, never trespassing upon, never victimizing the wife of his bosom, and mother of his babes. We have romance before marriage we want more chivalry in marriage.

This is not the world's morality, yet it seems to me the world must respect it. This high and pure Christian morality is not always enforced by Christian ministers, some of whom yield too much to human sensuality and depravity, instead of maintaining the higher laws of Christian purity which is but Nature restored or freed from its stains of sin. The world requires that unmarried women should be chaste, while it gives almost unbridled license to men. A girl detected in amours is disgraced and often made an outcast. In young men such irregularities are freely tolerated. They are "a little wild;" "they sow their wild oats;" but open profligacy, the seduction of innocence, the ruin of poor girls, adultery, harlotry and its diseases do not hinder men from marrying, nor from requiring that those they marry should have spotless reputations. It is not for a moment

87

permitted that women in these matters should behave like men; and a pure girl is given to the arms of a wasted debauchee, and her babes are perhaps born dead, or suffer through life with syphilitic diseases, while she endures a long martyrdom from disordered, diseased, and unrestrained sensuality. For the unmarried young men, soldiers, sailors, and all who do not choose to bear the burdens of a family, society has its armies of prostitutes women like others, and more than others, or in less reputable fashion, the victims of the unbridled lust of man. These are everywhere tolerated as "necessary evils," and, in some places, protected or regulated, and from economical or philanthropic considerations, or both, combined efforts are made to free them from the contagious diseases, which for some centuries have been a curse attending this form of the violation of the laws of nature one of the consequences of lust, which is the divorce of the sexual instinct from its natural use and purpose.

The Christian law of marriage, as set down in the Holy Scriptures, and defined by the best writers on moral theology, is in harmony with nature in consonance with the higher nature of man. "God hath set the earth in families." Adultery is a sin, because it disorders that divine arrangement. Selfish lust is a sin, because it mars it. Fornication is a sin, because it prevents pure marriages. Prostitution is a sin, because it is a sacrifice of women, who might be wives and mothers, to the selfish lusts of men. All useless indulgence is a waste of life, and a kind of suicide. In a pure marriage union men and women unite themselves with God in acts of creative power.

The progress of humanity depends upon individual development, and the conditions of generation and gestation. With culture, and a harmonized development, we acquire a higher and more integral life. When two parents are in their highest condition, and in a true union with each other, the child combines the best qualities of both parents. When parents are not in the unity of a mutual love, the child may be inferior to either parent. The intensity of mutual love tends to the reproduction of the best faculties of both parents in the child. When men or women are exhausted or diseased, the race deteriorates. Health is therefore one of the conditions of progress.

"It is all very fine," I shall be told, "to talk of purity and chastity; but we must take men as they are. How are you going to make men pure and chaste, and respectful of the purity of a woman? How can you get men with strong amative propensities to live like anchorites?"

How can you get men to do any right thing or refrain from any wrong thing? There are three motives: fear of punishment, hope of reward, and sense of right, or the principle of duty. The first of these is the lowest, but often the most effectual; the second is higher, and appeals to hope and the love of happiness; the third, the highest of all motives, pure and unselfish as the love of truth, as in mathematics, acts on noble minds with great power. Men of real conscientiousness love the right for its own sake. They are just from love of justice pure from a sense of love of purity. They love good, and God as the source of all good; and do right, not from fear or hope, but from pure love.

We must appeal to all motives. Men refrain from theft and other dishonest conduct from the dread of disgrace and punishment; because they see that "honesty is the best policy," and from a sense of justice and regard to the rights of property, or a sense of honor which makes a mean action impossible. By similar motives great numbers are restrained from drunkenness and other vices. Children are to be restrained from impurity by the fear of the terrible consequences of unnatural indulgence in causing disease and pain, by the hope of a pure, healthy, and happy life of love in manhood and womanhood, and by a sense of the beauty and holiness of chastity, and the sacredness of the functions by which the race is re-created and preserved. The religious feelings that our bodies are to be kept pure, healthy, and holy in every way as "the temples of the Holy Ghost," cannot be too early instilled into the infant mind, which is open to the highest sentiments of veneration, devotion, and heroic religion. In youth there are the same motives. Indulgence in solitary vice is self destructive of all that youth most values, a profanation of his own body. Seduction is a desecration of what he should hold in the most tender reverence. To the young man, womanhood should be sacred, and every woman, mother, sister, the beloved of the present or the future, should never be wronged by one thought of impurity. In this matter instinct goes with right. The inward voice supports the outer law of morality. Before men can become bad, their instinctive modesty must be broken down. Unless very badly born, with disordered amativeness hereditary from a diseased and lustful parentage, they must be perverted and corrupted before they can act immodestly and impurely.

Women are protected by a strong public sentiment around them. They have the dread of disgrace. For them to yield to their own affectionate desires, or the solicitations of a lover, is a fall, is ruin. They have the hope of a loving husband, a happy home, and the respect of society. And in women passion has commonly less force, and the sentiment of modesty and purity more power. Women are weak in yielding to solicitation, giving everything for love; but we see how protective of female virtue are these motives to vast numbers.

Men can perfectly restrain the sensual part of their natures whenever and wherever they have a strong motive to do so. A child would be simply mad who was not controlled by the presence of father, mother, or persons he respected or feared. Young men have no difficulty when they are in company of pure women. They are in no trouble where their lives are full of mental and muscular activity, and particularly if their habits of eating simply and temperately, or refraining from heating and exciting stimulants, and sleeping in cool beds and fresh air are such as health requires. There needs but the strong will to live purely in any one, and at any age the will that comes from the high motives of conscience and religion, or all motives combined. A strong sense of what is just and right controls even the motions of our bodies and actions which seem to be involuntary. A man who has a vivid sense of the right and duty of refraining from sensuality, and preserving his own purity of mind and body, and the chastity of all women, will do so even in his dreams. When the will is right, all things are soon brought into its subjection. The mind controls the organization, and the life forces are directed into other channels. A strong man, full of life and love, can safely hold a virgin in his arms and respect her virginity, if he have but the motives and the will to do so. If he be pure in his will, how can he commit impurity? If a woman be sacred in his eyes, how can he profane her? It is not that men have not the power of self-restraint, the power to do right, it is that they lack the motive. They have lost the sense of right; they are even impelled to do wrong by the pressure of opinion around them. Boys and young men are driven into libertinage by the ridicule of their companions. Vice is considered manly. They seek sensuality in an evil emulation, as they learn to smoke, or game, or drink. And, later on, vanity has often more to do with excess than the force of lust. Young men seduce girls that they may boast of it. They keep mistresses because it is the fashion. They exhaust themselves, because they wish to give a high idea of their manly prowess. Even in marriage women are injured, and have their health destroyed, yielding weakly, or from a false sense of duty, to a husband, whose own motive is the desire to acquit himself manfully in what he considers his marital duties. Men and women are, in thousands of cases, wretched victims to what they imagine to be the wants or expectations of each other. A man, ignorant of the nature of woman, and the laws of the generative function, goes on in a process of miserable exhaustion to please his wife; she submits, sometimes in pain, often in disgust, weariness, and weakness, to what she dare not from love or fear refuse.

Men have to know what is right, and the will to be right. This will is omnipotent. God helps those who have the will, who have even the desire to do right.

If the presence of those we fear or reverence, respect or love, restrain us from sin and stimulate us to right action, faith in the existence and presence of God and angels and the spirits of the departed, must have a more powerful and pervading influence. No one who really believes in the existence of a Supreme Being: no one who is strongly impressed with the reality of a Spiritual life, can go on doing what he knows to be wrong. A religious faith is therefore the most powerful of all restraints from evil and the incitement to good.

CHAPTER XII
The Parent's Influence in Determining
the Physical and Moral Status of His Children.

How universal is the desire to get married; it is the great end and aim of life. There may be no change, in every possible point of view, so necessary to be previously well considered as matrimony; but yet how paramount to all others in man's history is the incentive which leads us on. It is indeed a most fertile theme, and volumes have been dedicated to this subject alone. Our consideration herein of the question relates less to its obligations than its expediency, inasmuch as the main property of these remarks applies more to the issue than the individuals immediately concerned.

In thus premising that our reference is to the future and not to the past, it is useless repining at what we have made ourselves, except it be to let those who succeed us know the anguish we suffer for our own misdeeds, and by our representations induce them to avoid the hidden rocks on which we have foundered.

In advocating the guardianship of health, the father is held responsible for his child, not only for what he has made him, but also for what he may make of him. In this large world, however, three-fourths have to shift for themselves; this address, therefore, is expressly dedicated to such, in order that they may see what is due from themselves, and how to repair the neglect these pages may find them suffering from.

In tracing the sick or delicate health of a child, or a growing lad, or a young man, to parental origin, supposing the father or mother to be made sensible that such is the case that to themselves alone, or chiefly, have they to attribute their child's affliction, how painful must be their reflections! A parent's love for a child is the more active and fervent in proportion to such disadvantages, and therefore the more to be deplored is the calamity. A mother's grief and a father's regret, what can be more poignant, on witnessing their sinking or expiring offspring, especially when they know that, on giving it life, they conveyed to it the seeds of its premature dissolution? With such a fact constantly before us, how it behooves those anticipating unions to ponder before they perpetuate their own misery, if not for their own sakes and sufferings, at least in mercy to those who are to issue from their loins. What else can be expected from a couple where the combined health of the two is not equal to the ordinary health of one perfect individual? And how rarely do we really find, especially in all interesting matches, but that the bride or bridegroom is in what is termed "delicate health." Hence, oftentimes, the popular notion, that a pale-faced woman, or a "lovesick looking" young man, have only to marry to get well, instead of getting well first and marrying afterwards. A certain class of individuals are ever ready to ridicule this train of reasoning; but if they unhappily disregard its application, they will be sure to find out, when too late, the truth to fall at their own doors. Hence, if there be any truth in the statement, that children inherit the constitutions as well as the features and minds of their parents, the imperative and urgent necessity of young persons contemplating marriage, to look before they leap, not only at the trousseau of the wife's dowry, or the husband's estate and means, but at the stability of each other's health. It is true, marriage is oftentimes a remedy for certain ills, but only those ills begotten by a disregard of natures ordinances; for it is as much a law at a certain age that parties should marry, as that fishes should swim or birds should fly; but then marriage is only timely when consistently carried out with regard to age and condition. It is monstrous when particular deformities, or fatal, though lingering sickness, exist at an espousal.

We have talked of children inheriting disease and delicate health from their parents: the following facts are striking corroberations of how much, and principally in what way, children take after their fathers and mothers; how not only health, form and feature, but intellect and genius, or imbecility and viciousness may be propagated. The fact has been long observed and known, but only recently practically elucidated, and that most satisfactorily, by Mr. Alexander Walker. This gentleman has written extensively on matters connected with the subject, but the book, whence his views are taken, is entitled "Intermarriage." That portion under immediate notice relates to the resemblance of progeny to parents.

The idea that it is possible by appropriate marriages to secure a certain standard of beauty, statute and form, unfortunately does not secure that notice it is worthy of, because people rarely think of the possibility until courtship has commenced; but the evidence presently to be offered must convince the most skeptical and selfish that it is of most certain accomplishment, and, furthermore, that so attractive are the results, that the reflective will take care not to surrender their affections merely to love at sight, while it is quite possible to command that powerful feeling when well, equally as when ill-directed.

All parents, writes Mr. Walker, communicate distinct points of resemblance to their children, and the part which each parent takes is modified by the similarity or dissimilarity betwixt father and mother. For instance, in unions between person of the same variety, such as where a similarity in complexion, form, make, and temperament exists, certain fixed resemblances ensue in the issue thereof. Again, when persons of different complexion and different temperaments marry, the issue partake of different points of resemblance. Lastly, when persons of the same family (breeding in and in, as it is termed,) marry, the issue assume new features; he therefore divides his investigations of resemblances betwixt parents and children into three varieties which are as follows:

Firstly, when persons of the same variety marry, but of different families.

Secondly, where persons of the opposite variety marry, also of different families.

Thirdly, where persons of the same family intermarry.

In the first arrangement, where persons of the same variety marry, one parent communicates the Anterior series of resemblances, and the other the Posterior; but either parent may impart either series. The Anterior series consist of the Forehead, and bony part of the face, as

| The Orbits | Jaws, |
| Cheek Bones | Chin and Teeth, |

as well as the shape of the organs of sense, and the tone of the voice, and likewise the whole of the internal nutritive system which signifies the contents of the trunk, such as the lungs, heart, and digestive organs, as well as the form of the trunk.

The Posterior series consists of the Back-head, the few more moveable parts of the face and the locomotive system, as

| The external Ear | Lower part of the Nose, |
| Under Lip | Eyebrows, |

and the external forms of the body in so far as they depend on the muscles, as well as the form of the limbs, even to the fingers, toes, nails, etc.

Mr. Walker assigns reasons why certain organizations should go together, namely, from their connexion; such as, for instance, he says, that portion of the brain which regulates the senses corresponds with them and consequently influences their organization internal and external, and, in like manner, that portion influencing the motive powers, namely the back-head, influences the form of the limbs and hence the resemblance to that parent in those particulars which imparts either series.

Various corroborations are found in Mr. Walker's book to prove the assertion. It has been observed that in a female with a short and round face, chubby cheeks, and a full forehead, but "contracted and fine in the nose and mouth," the trunk will be found wide and capacious and the limbs tapering; whilst, on the contrary, women with slender oval faces and aquiline noses, have spare and slender bodies.

With a view of determining the truth of the statement of either parent giving a particular series of resemblances of themselves to their offspring, Mr. Walker recommends the various parts of the head and face of a child, as detailed in the subjoined columns, to be examined, and those points not possessed by the child as resembling either father or mother to be crossed out, and those resembling to remain, when it will at once be seen which parent the child takes after, and from which the anterior or posterior series is derived.

Parts resembling the Mother	Parts resembling the Father
Forehead.	Forehead
Upper middle part of head	Upper middle part of head
Bony parts of face	Bony parts of face
Teeth	Teeth
Digestive System	Digestive System
Form of Eyes	*Form of Eyes*
Eyebrows, Point of Nose	*Eyebrows, Point of Nose*
Upper Lip, Under Lip	*Upper Lip, Under Lip*
Ears, Back-head	Ears, Back-head
Upper middle part of Head over the Ears and towards the Temples	Upper middle part of Head, over the Ears and towards the Temples
Frontal Protuberances	Frontal Protuberances
Chest, Limbs	Chest, Limbs
Fingers, Toes, Nails	Fingers, Toes, Nails

Those parts printed in italics are variable, by the cerebral (back part of the brain so called) influencing the muscles more or less connected with them.

In examining resemblances, the front face of a child may resemble one parent, but the profile will resemble the other.

The front view best displays the observing faculties; the profile view, the active ones.

"The parent who gives the locomotive system, does not give the carriage and the manner of walking. These are always given by the other parent, who gives the organs of sense." Therefore the child with the limbs in resemblance of the mother walks like the father, and vice versa, as the eye directs the walking and gives the character to it. Witness the step of the countryman, or the man of fashion. "The transmission of the mind is derived in equal parts from both parents, when parents are of the same variety, and the temper and disposition in like manner; but one gives the whole of the nutritive, and the other the whole of the locomotive organs."

The child who resembles the anterior series of the one

parent, is also characterized by a corresponding similarity in the functions of taste, smell, sight, etc., and also the observing, imitating, acquiring, and other faculties. The back-head, or posterior series, imparts the passions and appetites.

"Whatever increases the ardor of passion, invigorates the progeny" this shows the indispensability of health in parties marrying. The condition of health, the occupation, the state of mind, whether happy or saddened, at the period of matrimony, all have an influence upon the offspring. In the excitement present, whether it be intellectual or sensual, whether it be the gentle emotion of pure affection, or the burning passion of mere desire, how necessarily must the consequences fall upon the issue thereof.

How important, then, is it to select the most fitting period of life, when the intellect is ripest, when the health is most perfect, and when circumstances combine to diffuse the greatest happiness to bride and bridegroom; how important after what has been stated, that the mind and health of one parent and the appetites, passions and figure of the other, are perpetuated in the offspring, that the selection should be a judicious one, and made only with reflection and forethought?

We now come to the second variety, called, in agricultural phraseology, "The Law of Crossing," which is where parties marry who are of different temperament and characters. In the former instance, it was stated, that where the father and mother were of the same variety, either parent might communicate the resemblances which went together, namely, mind and health or the forehead and digestive organs, etc., and the back-head, or will or appetites and form of limbs, etc.

Now, where parties of different breeds marry, supposing them of equal age, vigor, etc., the MALE gives the back-head and locomotive organs, and the FEMALE the face and nutritive organs.

Hence, in "cross" alliances, the intellect of the mother, the animal power of the father, descend usually to the offspring, except in especial cases, which are explicable on the principle, that power imparts power, and debility, debility.

The inference from this statement is, that in healthy alliances with persons of different variety, the father gives the energy and the mother the intellect.

This is as it should be, and as such a union always commands like results (which marriage among the same variety do not, (for there either parent, be it remembered, may give either mind or strength), it follows that cross-breeds secure a more vigorous and healthy progeny, and hence are to be preferred.

There are sundry modifications observable, even in the resemblances thus given; but they do not upset the positive law, that the father (the amount of health being equal) gives the character of the frame, and the mother the organs of sense.

The last variety is where the parents are both of the same family where the propagation is termed 'breeding in and in.'

"The third law operates where both parents are not only of the same variety, but of the same family in its narrowest sense, and where the female gives ALWAYS the back-head and locomotive organs, and the male the face and nutritive organs," precisely the reverse of what takes place in crossing.

Agriculturists, sportsmen, cattle breeders, and all persons concerned in the rearing of animals, are well aware that in those kinds of unions the race degenerates; and our own species are not exempt from the same law. Every person can attest the fact, by observing among his friends where such unions are preserved, as cousins intermarrying, and other near relations, the evident falling off in the issue, if any rise at all.

An appendage as to these curious facts, Mr. Walker considers that the sex of the child is more usually determined by that parent imprinting the vital system, subject to some exceptions. The prolific power of either sex depends upon their relative state of health.

Thus, then, we observe the children take after their parents in equal proportions. A child will resemble its father in the back part of the head, and in that portion of the frame influenced by it, as the form and stature, whereas it will take after its mother in the front part of the head and the vital system, or in other words, the health and existence. Of course, these resemblances are modified by the relationship, as stated, existing betwixt the mother and father, whether they be of the same variety, or of the same family, or of entirely different characteristics. Marriages between parties of the same variety do not produce such decisive results as among those of opposite variety; and those among the same family are the least prolific and healthy of the range.

Now, it must be remembered that the parents giving the intellect and existence, or the energy and form, convey to their offspring the peculiarities of their own organization. The power of reproducing the species accompanies the vital system, and only in proportion to the perfection of the latter is the perfection of the former. Hence, if a parent, in infirm health, with peculiar nervous or other derangements, happens to perpetuate in his own child the anterior series namely, intellect and the nutritive system, what can be expected in the ensuing generation, should that child survive, or in his turn marry or become a parent? The same result would follow, and the degeneracy at last would end in the cessation or further extension, and the race of such would become extinct. To those who perfectly understand these remarks and their application, many circumstances connected with their own health become immediately explicable, which before were matters of wonderment, how such and such could be. The inference shows how dependent the negative system of man is upon the general health, and how much that rests upon ancestral origin.

CHAPTER XIII
Domestic Infelicity Its Causes and Its Cures

Matrimony is a condition congenial with our nature. It is a main incident in human happiness. Even the birds pair, and what a reproof that should be to all obstinate bachelors and old maids. Apart from the feelings which generate love, and which make men go through fire and water to obtain the object of their affection, and which urge women to leave happy and wealthy homes to realize their sympathy and devotion, there is a great feeling in the circumstance of the mere communion in the friendship betwixt man and wife, which can exist nowhere else in like degree; apart from the ties of offspring that may bless a union, the fact of the worldly partnership, and the necessary mutual confidence existing in all matters of domestic and political economy cement the compact and render marriage the fastest attachment in the world. Hence the delightful position, above all price, of a pair well and suitably allied to each other in marriage. Much is necessary to be known with a view to discriminate between evil and good; to foretell happiness or misery. How different are men's feelings on the subject at twenty and thirty. There is no trial beforehand of character and disposition. Marriage is a hit or miss; the shot when once fired cannot be recalled. Courtship is a very artificial criterion; the face is lighted up with its best smiles and wears the cleanest aspect, every flaw is concealed not a stray curl is suffered to hang out of place, the voice assumes its most melodious tones, the very gait is graceful, the picture is handsomely framed and the conquest is complete. Both sexes adopt the like maneuver, and both frequently disappoint each other.

"Men are April when they woo, December when they wed. Maids are May when they are maids, but the sky changes when they are wives."

Young people usually pride themselves upon being the best judges of what and who is most suitable. Courtship is an affair that advice is seldom sought in, and, should it be tendered, is rarely acceptable; it is hard to counsel upon, but the prudent will at least reflect, lest they be too precipitate, and should not disregard the counsel that persons authorized may tender. It is somewhat curious that all imaginative writers, such as romance manufacturers and novel concocters, represent fathers as obdurate and hard-hearted, and mothers as inimical generally to their children's choice. The notion is a false one and ill-timed; for who can feel such interest, such dear solicitude for their children's prosperity and happiness as the authors of their being?

What a void in an old man's heart is a disobedient and ungrateful child! How hard it is to regulate these matters! Young folks do not for a moment recollect that their parents may have been lovers and must have acquired some experience worth detailing. Certainly, an immensity depends on a good example being set at home, care in excluding unsuitable acquaintances for our children, caution and yet an interest in introducing others.

But the object I have entered upon is where the noose is tied, whence there is no escape whence all hope of a change, except that brought about by mutual or principal forbearance, is absent; I allude to domestic infelicity. Of course, there are a thousand and possible more provocatives to family jars and dissensions that can render married life a most formidable and continuous warfare.

What is the principal and provoking cause to marital infelicity to perpetual squabbles to family discomfort to neglect of home let us add, to ruin, desolation and beggary? We shall not be far wrong in attributing the majority of two especial common and prevalent vices, namely, drunkenness and irascibility of temper. In dividing them, in justice we must lay the blame of the former principally to the husband, the latter to the wife. Of course the tables are sometimes turned, and there are exceptions to both conditions. To these two evils I purpose confining my remarks and suggestion for their alterations, if not for their removal.

A man may take to drinking through want of comfort at home, and the woman may acquire a bad temper through a husband's neglect; it is impossible to go into the very many inquiries of the why, and how, and what is the cause; else we must canvass over personal dislikes, jealousies, opposing habits, physical inaptitudes, disparity of ages, family interpositions, &c. We come to this fact: hundreds and hundreds of men are drunkards, and thousands of women are plagued with terrible irascible dispositions. What is the remedy?

The companion to a drunken mate is the worst off, because the drunkard soon falls into that state of health that the stimulus comes to be his only support, and his physical condition is a hell to him without his soul-spoiling antidote; reason and reflection are of little use to a depraved habit. The consequences are the more likely to bring him to his senses, and these consequences are general bodily suffering, extreme ill-health, and loss of business. It is well, where friends and relatives will interpose and express their indignation and show their displeasure, and perhaps well-expressed contempt may create a thought at least towards reformation. Coercion, if the nearest of kin might use it would no doubt have great influence. Drunkenness had best be punished by positive imprisonment, and why not? Offences less injurious to public morals are, and what is the object, but to prevent their repetition? Thanks however, to the spirit of the age, inebriation is on the decline. It exists chiefly among the very ignorant and the badly brought up.

Now let us just view the consequences of irascibility of temper. I need not picture the dreariness or the constant confusion of a home beset by constant quarrels. That such things are, every day tells of them. If we read them not in the public journals, we learn of them through the travel of small talk through scandal and other channels, and many of us know more or less from nearer sources the truth of such a report.

In irascibility of temper, there are two things to be considered: By no means to aggravate it, and by all means to try and subdue it. In whomsoever the fault rests, the other should not fan the flame. Suppose we throw the blame on the weaker of the two sexes; the only alternative is to treat it with forbearance. A despairing man will dole out his lamentations to the effect that he is the most wretched of all living creatures that he has no peace that the maxim so often broached is reversed, and whatever is, is wrong "that his wife has the most turbulent, restless, dissatisfied, worst temper in the world" that she either sulks or raves that no cat and dog were ever such bitter antagonists as his spouse and himself; his very detail provokes a smile, but alas, it is too true, and his position is indeed a most miserable one. An indignant man will exclaim he would not put up with it; he would soon show who was master. Such a feeling, such a disposition, and such a mode of proceeding is rarely successful. In the struggle for mastership hard words lead to fisticuffs, tearing of caps, and abusive language, language bad to use and worse to utter before children. As well attempt to quench fire with oil, or carry water in a sieve, as to subdue the temper of a willful woman by hard means, such as by her own weapon an unruly tongue. Irascibility is temporary insanity. And a woman when thus wild and ungovernable is unquestionably mad. And how altered now is the treatment of the insane; straitjackets, belts, iron bands, hand-cuffs, and wooden stocks, are supplanted by mild physical restraint, gentle persuasion, and every possible show of kindness. It will do the heart good to learn that humanity and benevolence and generous forbearance, with coaxing and solicitation firmly exercised, have entirely superseded the lash, the threat and (one can happily add) the torture of by-gone times. "Have a wife and rule a wife" makes a good comedy where the parts are set down, but the acting is not modeled in nature. No wife should take advantage of this advice and refer to these hints to husbands as sanctioning her viciousness or disposition, for the remarks may apply to herself, and be as practically in request by her companion; but the benedict may rely upon it that forbearance is his best shield of defense: the attacks rebound from it. An angry and contentious woman will have the last word, and so long as the husband provokes the argument, so long will it be kept up. Never mind the sharp hit of a wife's malice; so long as you know you do not deserve them, you can afford to bear them. If you are well aware that keeping the dinner waiting, staying out past your time, introducing smoking in your parlor, having noisy friends who provoke you to stay up late, giving bachelor parties, offend and bring upon you all the domestic uneasiness possible, all I can say is, you are very foolish to do these things, and after all, you can easily abandon such practices without much detriment to yourself. If your mind be the stronger of the two, and you value peace and quietness at home, cultivate pursuits more pleasing to your wife, and you will most likely ensure your object; this kind of forbearance will be certain to succeed in the long run. Husbands cannot expect to have everything their own way; they must give and take; they may talk of their supremacy, their being the prop of the house, the support of the family and they will live to be asked by the wife, who else should be? So it goes for nothing, and the man had best hold his tongue.

No my friend, if you are a melancholy, hypchondriacal, and yet disputattious man and have a disputatious spitfire of a wife, I do not envy you your position; but of this I am sure, and I have seen a great deal of it although I do not confess to be a party to the drama, that kindness, concession, and quiet reasoning, and, if that won't do, generous forbearance is the only loophole of escape you have. If, madam supposing my reader to be a lady the remarks apply to yourself, as the self-willed or the abused, pray interpret good naturedly my suggestions. I am an advocate for a woman's rights, and I contend that a husband should be respected. I abhor oppression and cruelty and would recommend no one to tamely submit to be trampled upon, but I know the virtue of concession, and the value of mutual forgiveness. Most irascible people are otherwise amiable and benevolent.

In Montgomery's "Law of Kindness" is given an anecdote of an irascible man denying himself to a Quaker, whom he at the same time abused by the epithet of "rascal," bidding him begone. The Quaker mildly replied, "Well, my friend, may God put thee in a better mind." The angry man was subdued by the kindness of the reply, and, after a careful consideration, became convinced he was wrong. He sent for the Quaker, and after making a humble apology, he said, "How were you able to bear my abuse with so much patience?" "Friend," replied the Quaker, "I will tell thee. I was naturally as violent and hot as thou art; but I knew that to indulge my temper was sinful and also very foolish. I observed that men in a passion always spoke very loud, and thought if I could control my voice, I should keep down my passion. I therefore made a rule never to let it rise above a certain key; and, by a careful observance of this rule, I have, with the blessing of God, entirely mastered my natural temper." We may depend on it, kindness is the best rod. The Christian motto is: "Overcome evil with Good." If properly carried out, it is a key which opens the hearts of all around us, giving us a place in their affections. It will disarm anger of its power, hatred of its sting, enmity of its opposition, and sarcasm of its malice; it will make the communion of husband and wife more tender; it will secure the obedience of children; it will make the ties of friendship strong; it will turn enmity into benevolent feeling; it will minister to the widow and the orphan and the pitiless storms of winter; and it will look to the comfort of the dumb beasts who serve us, saving them from cruelty and ensuring them good treatment. All this it will do if practiced; if not the nearest road, it is the easiest way, to be Happy.

Lastly, if forbearance, if kindness, if, indeed, continued submission secures you no tranquility, resort at once to separation. If you cannot effect it by mutual consent, call in the aid of your nearest friends, and carry it out peremptorily. Let there be no truce; when once you resolve upon it, do it. A miserable home is bad for the wife, shocking for the family, and deplorable for the husband. By separation, surely, all the contention, and sparring, and jarring is at an end, and then our several philosophy must be to rest content; for, terrible as the isolation to a domestic party may be, it is much better than to be in perpetual war.

Thus far I have principally contended for the wife; thus far I have advised the husband to forego his authority and privileges; thus far I have contended for submission from the stronger to the weaker vessel, so that the lady cannot object to receive a parting word of advice to herself. Let every wife whose husband loves other places than his own home, or rather what should be his home, examine how far she imitates Peggy or Jenny. Jenny is all scepticism, and scarcely believes men can be honest; she doubts their fidelity, distrusts their steadiness of purpose, and anticipates nought but beggary and want.

"O heaven! Were man
But constant, he were perfect; that one error
Fills him with faults."
Such she believed awaited her choice, and thus she bid
"Dear Meg, be wise, and live a single life,
Truth, it's nae mows to be a married wife."
Peggy draws a livelier picture of the married state. She believes a
husband may be won to constancy: she thinks, if he errs,
"It's ten to ane the wives are maist to blame."
She places great faith in
"A bleezing ingle and a clean hearth stane."
And, last of all, she exclaims, inclusive of the hest efforts to
attract and please--
"Good humour and white begonets shall be
Guards to my face to keep his love for me."

Doubtlessly, these are sinister contrivances to win a
man's heart. The idea at once brings to the mind the delights of
our "ain fireside."
"Blest winter nights! When, as the genial fire
Cheers the wide hall, our cordial family
With soft domestic arts the hours beguile."

The disposition would impel me, in the pleasing
thoughts of such a scene, to disbelieve a woman wanting in her
contribution to so much comfort; but we gather knowledge as we
move along, and facts are too numerous to leave a doubt about it.
Katherine (the subdued wife of Petruchio) thus breaths her
recantation, and advises one of her own sex in the following
strain. It expresses all that can be said on such an occasion, and
husbands might club together to have a series of cards printed
with the admonition thereon, for presentation to unruly wives:
The Wife's Duty to her Husband.
"Fie, fie! unknit that threatening unkind brow;
And dart not scornful glances from those eyes,
To wound thy lord, thy king, thy governor;
It blots thy beauty, as frosts bite the meads;

107

Confounds thy fame, as whirlwinds shake fair buds;
And in no sense is meek or amiable.
A woman moved is like a fountain troubled,
Muddy, ill-seeming, thick, bereft of beauty;
And while it is so, none so dry or thirsty
Will deign to sip, or touch one drop of it.
They husband is thy lord, thy life, thy keeper,
 Thy head, thy sovereign; one that cares for thee
And for thy maintenance, commits his body
To painful labor both by sea and land;
To watch the night in storms, the day in cold,
 While thou liest warm at home, secure and safe
And craves no other tribute at thy hands
But love, fair looks, and true obedience;--
Too little payment for so great a debt.
Such duty as the subject owes the prince,
Even such a woman oweth to her husband;
And when she's froward, peevish, sullen, sour,
And not obedient to his honest will,
What is she but a foul, contending rebel,
And graceless traitor to her loving lord?--
I am ashamed that women are so simple
To offer war where they should kneel for peace!
Or seek for rule, supremacy, and sway,
When they are bound to serve, love, and obey."

CHAPTER XIV
Venereal or Sexual Diseases

Of the multitude of diseases which the human frame is liable to, none cause so much misery, moral and physical, as those called venereal. Many a thoughtless youth has in a moment of temptation given way to his passions and thus filled his system with corruption, which may never leave him to the end of his life, or what is far worse, he has poisoned the fountain of his life, he will leave it as a heritage of misery to his offspring or will taint the blood of the partner of his bosom making her the innocent partaker of his disease. How many such are there in every locality, dragging out a wretched existence, a misery to themselves and an eyesore to society. They are left, as it were, by the Almighty to warn others against vicious practices and point the moral of the preacher against vice and immorality.

Gonorrhea or Clap.

This is an inflammation of the mucous membrane of the sexual organs, accompanied by a discharge, the result of impure connection.

The symptoms of clap are as follows: shortly after the infection has been communicated, usually from three to eight days, a sensation of heat and uneasiness is experienced in the end of the penis, accompanied generally with a little redness and difficulty in passing water; in a day or two the discharge of matter increases, and becomes thinner and of a greenish or yellowish color, sometimes tinged with blood.

The head of the penis is red and inflamed, and the urine occasions a scalding pain. When the inflammation extends to the bladder, there is a distressing desire to pass water, with a constant uneasiness about the testicles, and between the legs. When the inflammation is high it produces what is called chordee, in which the penis is in a state of erection, and is curved downward with great pain; this occurs generally when the patient is warm in bed.

From the inflammation, phimosis may ensue, in which the foreskin is hard and swollen so that it cannot be drawn back;

or, when the swelling takes place behind the head it cannot be drawn forward and is called paraphimoses.

The glands of the groin sometimes swell and inflame, as well as the testicles.

Gleet is the result of gonorrhea, and proceeds into the chronic form, after active inflammation has subsided. It is sometimes very obstinate. Another result of gonorrhea is stricture, which is a partial closing up of the urethra, or passage leading from the bladder; this may be known by the stream of water becoming flattened or twisted like a gimlet, or forked.

Stricture causes much pain and inconvenience, and often, if not promptly cured, troubles the sufferer at various times during his whole life.

If the discharge be suffered to remain on the glans of the penis, or on the outside of the foreskin, excoriations, chaps and warts spring up speedily and plentifully, and protrude before the prepuce, or sometimes become adherent to it; therefore, this shows how necessary cleanliness is in these disagreeable complaints to escape the vexations alluded to. The earliest symptoms should always be attended to, and where there is the least suspicion that the disease has been contracted, (and all indulgence outside of wedlock is fraught with the greatest danger and risk), prompt and energetic action must be taken.

It is of the first importance to nip, if possible, the disease in its bud; and that this can be done frequently and successfully the adoption of the following method will prove.

Treatment: Immediately on the advent of the first symptoms, or as soon as there is reason to believe that the party must have received the infection, throw up an injection of the nitrate of silver. Take of nitrate of silver, 1 scruple; distilled water, 1 ounce, mix, and strain through blotting paper. Pour a small quantity of the solution into a wine-glass; procure a small glass syringe, fill the same with the preparation; carefully insert the point of the syringe into the urethra, and allowing the penis to rest loosely, press the piston of the syringe, and inject the contents. Hold the syringe still for half a minute to retain the solution in the urethra, and then suffer it to escape. There is generally some difficulty to a patient's applying an injection for the first time, and there is usually an apprehension lest he force the injection into the bladder there is little fear of that occurring, first owing to the general awkwardness, and secondly, to the natural resistance which the introduction of a stimulating fluid to a sensitive and resistive passage meets with. If the least pain or sense of distention ensue, the best plan is to withdraw the syringe, supposing half the injection only to have been thrown up, and suffer the injected fluid to return, and then to apply the remainder. The disease being rarely seated beyond a couple of inches at the onset, there is no need of the injection higher up, but the use of injections generally, as it is just possible that an injection might enter the bladder and it might not be advisable that it should go there, the pressure of the finger against the Perineum, during the operation, will prevent any fluid passing that spot. The introduction of a syringe, if carefully resorted to, seldom gives any pain; the orifice of the urethra is of course tender, and no violence should be used, and it is as well to dip, previously, the point of the syringe in a little sweet oil. On the withdrawal of the syringe and escape of the injection, a slight burning sensation is experienced, which soon subsides, and no further inconvenience is occasioned, until called upon to urinate, when a smart scalding is felt, and the last few drops of urine may bring a spot or two of blood. Succeeding to or before the act of micturition, if it be long deferred, there occurs rather a copious yellow discharge, which is given off from the membrane of the urinary passage in consequence of the injection, and is not to be considered as gonorrheal matter. This may be continued more or less for some hours, but it generally subsides into a thin watery secretion. The pain in passing water also goes off, and by night time or the following morning the effects of the injection have subsided. If the operation of the injection is ineffectual, the gonorrheal discharge will, in all probability, rapidly succeed, and with it the usual sensations of scalding and pain. It may happen to the contrary the gonorrheal symptoms may not have advanced, and there may still remain the red and tender orifice with a slight weeping. It is then prudent to repeat the injection, which will be accompanied by the like result as before, but possibly less acute. Supposing the symptoms of the Clap not to advance and yet not wholly to subside, the operation may be repeated once more. If, despite this third trial, much irritation ensue, with great heat on urinating, or itching after it, and it be attended with pain about the perineum, groin, or loins, or testicles, or no amendment be perceptible, the injection had better not be repeated, and the next and best step is immediately to relieve the bowels by a full dose (1 ounce) of castor oil, and to follow the action of the medicine by immersion in a warm bath, availing also of frequent local hot fomentations, and then to treat the disease the ordinary way.

If, happily, as it very frequently does, the injection annihilate the complaint a warm bath or two a day or two's quiet, with temperate living (local support, by means of suspensory bandage), and the avoidance of all stimuli, will find the patient perfectly convalescent.

If this treatment does not stop the disease, recourse must be had to other means to be used promptly.

A warm bath should be taken every second or third day. A suspensory bandage should be worn, the bowels kept open with castor oil and rest of body and mind strictly enjoined.

The common drink should be of the mildest diluents. Barley water and flax seed tea are the best drinks. Gruel is the next best repast; it will do for the evening, and makes an excellent supper. Indeed, in very severe instances, gruel is the only nourishment that should be taken for several days.

Drinks should be of the simplest kind, such as will pass the more readily through the kidneys, and produce the mildest urine; hence, next to water, have we milk and water, weak tea, barley water, flax seed tea, gum water or gum arabic (the best quality) may be suffered to dissolve in the mouth, not exceeding an ounce or two in the day, for it is not very digestible, but with the common drinks swallowed from time to time, it unites, and possibly renders the urine less acrid. The various light soups are permissible such as vermicelli, macaroni, tapioca, and gruel broth. Sweets, pastries, solid dumplings, plum-puddings, cakes, and all those sorts of things are bad. The bread should be taken toasted and eaten cold; or it may be sopped in warm tea, or warm milk. Porridge is not objectionable. The best bread, also, is the unfermented; and then, again, the "brown" is preferable to the "white." It helps to keep the bowels open, acts favorably on the kidneys, and at the same time, is very nourishing and palatable. Rusks, brown bread, biscuits and all the light farinaceous preparations are good. All salted meats, savory dishes, little surprises of delicacies, and "tit bits" must be avoided. The next and best help is bodily rest.

If a man could lay up for a week, it would nearly cure him. That, in ninety-nine cases out of a hundred, is impossible.

Scalding.

Keep the bowels open with castor oil, and take the following sedative mixture.

Mucilaginous and Sedative Mixture: Take of Bicarbonate of Potass., 1 drachm; Mucilage of Acacia, 3 ounces; Spirits of Sweet Nitre, 2 drachms; Tincture of Henbane, 3 drachms; Syrup of Tolu, 3 drachms; Distilled water, 4 ounces. Mix. Take three table-spoonful three times daily, morning, noon, and night.

Purgation always relieves the scalding. Bathing the penis in warm water, as warm as it can well be borne, will ease the smarting in passing urine; and if that fail, cold water may be found more effectual. Throwing up, before urinating, a syringeful of sedative injection, will help to allay the pain.

Sedative Injection to allay the Scalding and Pain: Take Extract of Belladonna, 10 grains; Plain or Rose water, 12 ounces. Mix. Throw up a syringeful frequently in the day.

Surfacial Discharge, and Ulceration of Glans, Prepuce, etc.

Where the discharge is traceable only to the Glans or Prepuce, and is or is not accompanied by cuticular excoriation, the application of a solution of Nitrate of Silver will, in one or two "brushings," put a stop to the secretions, and the "abrasive" invasion.

Solution of Nitrate of Silver: Take of Nitrate of Silver 1/2 drachm; Distilled Water, 1 ounce. Mix and strain through blotting paper. To be used with the feather end of a pen.

Solution of Sulphate of Zinc. Take of Sulphate of Zinc, 1 scruple;

Pure Water, 1 pint. Mix. Throw up between the nut and the foreskin a syringeful of this application two or three times daily.

To return to the treatment of the discharge. As soon, however, as the scalding is on the wane, then may be taken the various preparations of Copaiba, Cubebs, and other particular remedies, which now, for the benefit of the patient, a series of prescriptions are offered, the headings of which will guide to their selection.

The ordinary Capsules of Copaiba.

Three may be taken three times daily, to be swallowed as boluses; some people cannot take pills, but by merely half filling the mouth with water, and then throwing in what is to be swallowed, one gulp will take the whole down. This form of Copaiba spares the palate from the nauseous flavor of the medicine.

Cubebs.

Cubebs have been held as, and oftentimes they are, useful in gonorrhea. From two to three drachms of the Powder of Cubebs may be taken three times daily in water, observing the adjuncts of occasional purgatives, bland drinks, baths, and rest. If, however, Cubebs do not produce a marked good in three or four days, it is useless continuing them.

Cubebs and Copaiba are both stimulants and diuretics, and, as far as we know, act on the mucous membranes; but if carried beyond a certain effect, they irritate the kidneys, and produce considerable derangement. The following are several good formulæ.

Copaibic and Cubebic Mixture: Take of Balsam Copaiba, 1 ounce; Mucilage of Acacia, 3 ounces; Powder of Cubebs, ½ ounce; Spirits of Sweet Nitre, 2 drachms; Paregoric, 2 drachms; Simple Syrup, ½ ounce; Peppermint water sufficient to form a half pint mixture. Take two tablespoonfuls twice or thrice daily.

Compound Copaibic Mixture: Take of Honey, 1 ounce; Balsam Copaiba, 1 ounce; Powder of Acacia, 1 ounce; Liquor of Potass., 1 drachm. Mix, and add a little water gradually. Then take Tincture of Buchu, 1 ounce; Tincture of Cubebs, 1 ounce; Tincture of Opium, 30 drops. Peppermint and cinnamon water sufficient to form a half-pint mixture. Take one or two tablespoonfuls in a little water, two or three times daily. These are two excellent mixtures.

The Balsam Copaiba: May be taken in doses of a tea-spoonful simply floated on water, or may be taken in half a glass of sherry. It may be made with magnesia into pills, and ten to thirty swallowed in a day.

Preparation of Copaiba: Copaiba is often prepared in the form of tincture and various other solutions (in an alkaline form among the rest), all of which are severally good; it is at best a nauseous preparation, and if it disagree, is apt to throw out over the body a species of nettle-rash, that is very irritable, and often alarming to a patient, who considers it to be a fearful advance of the disease; a suspension of the medicine, a dose of physic, and a warm bath or two, will completely put a stop to it. The copaiba must be recurred to very cautiously, or suspended entirely in case of a relapse.

Pain and Difficulty in Passing Urine, with Irritability of the Bladder, etc., and frequent Desire to Urinate.

These are the natural consequences of extended inflammation. They often occur from other causes than Clap; but with it they are rarely entirely absent.

These maladies are often aggravated as the discharge diminishes, or rather, the severer they are, the discharge becomes more or less suspended, Nature seldom allowing two diseases to proceed with equal virulence at the same time. The remediatory measures are principally sedatives, demulcents, baths, and rest. Where a hardness or a tumor of the Perineum is present, leeches, warm fomentations, bran and other poultices are indispensable. Cupping is an expeditious and cleanly mode of relief in the earlier stages of severe pain thereabout.

Painful Micturation and Frequent Desire to Urinate.

Take of Camphor Julep, 8 ounces, Laudanum, 30 drops.

115

Mix. Take three tablespoonfuls three times daily.

Demulcent Drink to facilitate the Flow of Urine: Take of Barley-water, 2 pints; Nitrate of Potass, 2 scruples; White Sugar, 2 or 3 lumps. Mix. Take a wine-glassful three or four times daily.

If the case resists the means recommended, and symptoms increase, medical aid must be called in.

Inflammation of the Bladder Prostrate Gland.
Disordered Urine.

This is so far beyond the control of a non-medical invalid, that it is scarcely prudent to allude to it; but the symptoms may be told to urge the employment of the professional man.

Inflammation of the mucous lining of the bladder is marked by the whey-looking appearance of the urine and pain in urinating; frequent desire to empty the bladder; pain about the situation of it, and considerable fever. The Prostrate Gland and neck of the bladder become involved frequently in the disturbance, and present similar accompaniments, with the addition of great suffering in the perineum and rectum, a most pressing desire to void water, and yet inability to eject more than a drop or two at a time. Leeches, bleeding, and general active treatment, are in immediate requisition in such cases.

Chordee.

This is a most painful affection and is only present then the penis is distended or erect. When bleeding occurs, which it frequently does, it arises from some little vessel in the urinary passage giving way. The speediest way of deriving relief is by immersing the penis in cold water or wrapping linen rags dipped in the same, around the virile member. The pain is so intense, and the erection so constant when warm in bed, and the parts so very irritable, that the patient cannot sleep, and therefore it is advisable to administer sleeping draught and also to dip some lint in the embrocation and apply it to the under surface of the penis, going to bed with it on.

Sleeping Draught: Take of Solution of Acetate of Ammonia, ½ ounce; Camphor Julep, 1 ounce; Spirits of Sweet Nitre, ½ drachm; Tincture of Henbane, 1 drachm. Mix, for a draught taken at bed time.

The Embrocation Poison: Take of Opodeldoc, ½ ounce; Laudanum, ½ ounce. Mix. Label it "POISON" and use it as advised taking care it be not swallowed by mistake for the draught.

In obstinate cases of Chordee, leeches applied over the part will do good. The warm bath before going to bed will sometimes keep off the local excitement, and thereby allow sleep.

A pill composed of Camphor, 5 grains, and Belladonna, ½ grain, taken at bed time is highly beneficial.

Chordee will continue some time, and very much harass the individual, inducing frequently nocturnal emissions. Patience and persistence in the means suggested are the best antidotes.

Swelling of Prepuce, Phymosis.

A mere temporary enlargement is of no moment, although it shall attain treble or four times its ordinary bulk. In this instance, the Prepuce assumes a dropsical appearance, like a thin bladder filled with water, and is occasioned by what medical men call extravasated serum being deposited in the reticular membrane.

The treatment consists in the constant application of cold water by means of lint moistened therewith and applied thereon taking care to keep the penis well supported, rather than pendant. Syringing between the Prepuce and Glans with luke warm water, milk and water, will help to subdue the inflammation. The swelling mostly subsides after a little while; where ulcerations exist on the glans, or warts are progressing, and fear is entertained lest a permanent adhesion between the foreskin and nut shall take place, then division, as the lesser of two evils, is necessary.

Bubo

Buboes occur in gonorrhea, especially where there is any

external irritation or excoriation around the glans. They consist of a slight swelling of the glands in the groin, but they really lead to abscesses, and consequently are termed Sympathetic; they subside usually with the provoking cause. Warm fomentations, warm baths, and mild opening medicine are all that is required.

Swelled Testicles.

Diseases of the testicles are so fraught with after-mischief, that the most prompt and skillful attention should be sought after. Immediately on discovery of a swelled testicle, the first step should be to procure a suspender; it gives instantaneous relief. The warm bath is also valuable and indispensable, and may be resorted to daily.

The next and speediest way of relieving swelled testicle is by bleeding from the arm or cupping in the loins, observing the strictest rest and abstinence. Some physicians advise emetics, all recommend purgatives; and saline aperients are most effectual. If bleeding and cupping be dispensed with, leeches can scarcely be withheld but it is useless to apply them, except in large numbers. Frequent warm fomentations give great relief. The diet must be spare during this process, avoiding all wines, beer and spirits. Let the patient secure as much bed-rest as possible. Let him also ride rather than walk when he can, and sit rather than stand. About the second or third day, when the inflammation shall have reached its height, still observing the same precautions, use the Absorbent Mixture and keep up the secretion of the bowels. The testicles, or rather the scrotum, may be smeared or washed over, by means of a camel-hair brush, with the Tincture of Iodine (procure an ounce in a stopper vial); the operation will occasion some smarting, but it is only of very short duration. The application must be repeated night and morning, until the skin exfoliates, or becomes too painful to be borne. As soon as the surface admits of re-application, it must be renewed until the swelling disappears.

Absorbent Mixture. Take of iodide of potass ½ drachm; distilled water, 7½ ounces; tincture of henbane, 2 drachms; simple syrup,

2 drachms; mix. Take three tablespoonfuls three times daily. Each fresh bottle of mixture may have 10 grains extra of the iodide of potass.

GLEET.

Gonorrhoea proceeds from sexual intercourse and is infectious; but it may arise from a variety of other causes, drinking, sexual excesses, whether with females or from masturbation, accident, or ill-health. Gleet is a subdued inflammation of the same kind, possessing more or less all the properties of the former, although not so determinately infectious. Is Gleet curable? Unquestionably it is but by no specific Balsam, Elixir, or especially Simple. It must be treated with reference to the existing symptoms. It has to be repeated and told, that the drainage is kept up by local irritation, by a loss of tone in the secreting vessels, by such a thing as sympathy with some neighboring or remote infirmity. This local irritation may be removed by local application. There is a time when the mildest injections are promptly successful, whilst at others a cure only awaits the use of very active ones.

The patient may make his selection of the annexed formulae.

Caustic Injection. Nitrate of silver, 4 grains; water, 1 ounce. Mix.

Sulphate of Zinc and Tannin Injection. Sulphate of zinc, 8 grains; Tannin, 1 scruple; water, 5 ounces. Mix.

Chloride of Zinc Injection. Chloride of zinc, 6 grains; soft water, 2 ounces. Mix; this is very serviceable in obstinate cases.

Tonic Drops. Take of tincture of sesquichloride of iron, ½ ounce; disulphate of iron, 30 grains; tincture of cantharides, 1 drachm; distilled water, 3 ounces; simple syrup, ½ ounce. Mix. Take a teaspoonful twice daily in a little water.

Turpentine Pills. Pills made of Canada turpentine, rolled up with licorice powder. Two, three, or four may be taken twice daily.

Tonic Pills. This is a very nice pill. Take of sulphate of iron, composition Kino powder, Venice turpentine, extract of gentian, each ½ drachm. Mix and divide into 24 pills. Take 1, two, or three four times daily.

Aperient Pills. During the persistence of tonic and stimulating medicines, the bowels may be kept open by any mild laxative. The following pill or pills will do. Take of compound of rhubarb pills, 6 grains each. 1 or 2 for a dose.

CHANGING THE REMEDIES.

Upon the principles of "trying something else" is often advantageous; for it is useless repeating what has been found unsuccessful; and it is folly to throw up our endeavors, particularly when it is shown the disease rarely cures itself.

If the Gleet proceeded from disordered or acrid urine, the attention must be directed to that secretion. The drinks and diet, as in the earlier stages of gonorrhoea, must be adhered to. The warm bath and rest must come in also for a share of the treatment. Where there is reason to believe that general debility has become hypochondriacal, it is admirable to try a change of air and scene.

STRICTURE OF THE URETHRA.

Of all diseases of the genito-urinary system, stricture must be allowed to be the most terrible. It is not the most difficult to cure; but it involves, when neglected, more serious disturbances disturbances which frequently terminate only with loss of life. Stricture is a disease unfortunately of extensive prevalence; and in nine cases out of ten is the sequence of local irritation, consequent generally upon gonorrhoea or gleet. The first indications are the lengthened time required in urinating, the act is not performed so cleanly as it used to be; the stream differs in its flow, seldom comes out full and free, but generally split into three or four fountain-like spirts.

At other times, it twists into a spiral form, and then suddenly splits into two or three more streams, whilst at the same moment the urine drops over the person or clothes, unless great care be observed.

In advanced cases, the urethra becomes so narrow, and the bladder so loses its power to expel the urine forward, that it then falls upon the shoes or trousers, or between them.

120

In the next attack which is very difficult to avert, the patient finds he cannot complete the act of making water without several interruptions, each attended with a painful desire resembling that induced by too long retention of that fluid.

With respect to the change consequent upon permanent stricture, dissection enables us in some degree to arrive at the truth. Excrescences and tubercles have been found growing from the wall of the urethra; but in the majority of instances, the only perceptible change is a thickening of the canal here and there of indefinite length; but whether it be occasioned by the exudation of coagulate lymph, or whether it be the adhesion of ulcerated surfaces, which I contend are more or less present in gleet, is not so easy to determine; at all events it is undoubtedly the result of inflammation of the urethra.

Fig. 42, untitled>>

Spasmodic stricture is generally seated at the neck of the bladder, and may occur to persons in good health from exposure to wet or cold; from some digestive derangement; from long retention of urine, particularly while walking, owing to the absence of public urinals; or to violent horse exercise; but more frequently does it happen to those young men who, when suffering from gleet or gonorrhoea, imperfectly or perfectly cured, commit excesses in diet or drink. Stricture may also be caused by injuries, by falling, blows, wounds, and also by masturbation.

The following diagrams are further explanatory of stricture in its various forms.

Figs. 43 to 52>>

The dark marginal lines denote the calibre of the urethra, and the thin inner lines the actual diameter of the obstructed passage. Fig. 43 shows the stricture to be on the upper part of the urethra, Fig. 44, the lower part. Fig. 45 exhibits a stricture of some length, and a somewhat contracted state of the whole canal. Fig. 46 denotes a very common form of stricture, which resembles a bag tied in the middle; it is the least difficult to cure, because it signifies that the seat of irritation is limited; but these cases are generally precursory to severer forms, if not promptly attended to. Fig. 47 represents a stricture of considerable length, and of course very difficult of removal. The clumsy introduction of a bougie, or, in other instances, the unjustifiable introduction of one, is likely to, and very frequently does, lacerate the delicate and irritable membrane, and make a false passage. Fig. 48 exhibits an instance in numbers 1 and 2; number 3 shows a false passage made by a bougie, and on obliteration of the ordinary passage of the urethra, the result of inflammation, constituting an impassable stricture; the lower figure exhibits a false opening made, in the first instance, by a fruitless effort at passing an instrument, when inflammation completed the process. No urine escaped from it, of course; because communication was cut off from the bladder by the impassable stricture, the outlet for the discharge of that fluid being through a sinuous opening marked 2; 3 denoting the closed end of the urethra. Fig. 49 exhibits a stricture, where the posture part was enlarged by the constant pressure of urine to escape through the narrowed part of the urethra; ulceration ensued, and a fistulous opening was the consequence; the stricture was seated high up, and the fistulous canal was several inches long, terminating in the upper and posterior part of the thigh; the urine used to dribble through it as well as through the urethra. In Fig. 50 is presented an illustration of extensive ulceration producing two fistulous openings; the state of the urethra was only discovered after death. Fig. 51 portrays irregular and extensive ulceration. Fig. 52 shows an impervious urethra, and a fistulous opening, through which the urine flowed.

TREATMENT.

Stricture, if early attended to, is a disease easily remediable; if neglected, its horrors accumulate, and sufferings the most acute close the scene. Such, however, is the process of science, that it is almost possible to cure the most inveterate case at all events, to relieve it; but that is no reason why the initiatory notices should be disregarded. Stricture is of two kinds, spasmodic and permanent: the treatment of the first is chiefly medical, the treatment of the latter chiefly mechanical. The principal agents I rely upon, in the cure of the former, are the warm bath, rest, sedatives, and certain dietetic restrictions; for the removal of the latter I place unbounded confidence in the practice of dilatation.

One of the most powerful adjuncts in the treatment of all affections of the urethra, bladder, prostate gland, kidneys and other structures, pertaining to the urinary and generative system, is the warm bath.

The only mode of ascertaining the precise condition of the urethra is by an examination of it, which should not be delayed a moment after suspicion is entertained of the impending evil.

The course of dilatation is as follows: The seat of the stricture being ascertained, a bougie, somewhat larger than the calibre of the urinary current, warmed and dipped in an oleaginous mixture, combined with some sedative or stimulant, according to circumstances, is to be passed to the stricture, and the gentlest pressure employed for the space of five, ten, or twelve minutes, according to the irritation it produces, removing it as soon as any uneasiness is felt.

The bougie is to be pressed softly but steadily against the obstruction, now and then withholding for a minute the bearing, so as to allow a respite to the stretched membrane; the renewing, by what is better done than expressed, an "insinuating" pressure for the space of time advised above. The patient should not be dispirited, even if the bougie do not perforate the stricture at the first trial; it would doubtless do so, if longer time were employed but that is rarely advisable, except in cases where the urine can scarcely escape, or much expedition be requisite. Should the operation even be unsuccessful in the first attempt, the patient will find his ability to micturate much greater than before the introduction. A great advantage of the cure by dilatation, independently of its safety and efficacy, is the insignificant pain it occasions; the sensation produced being only like a pressing desire to make water, which immediately subsides on withdrawing the bougie.

An entrance having been gained, a bougie of a larger size is selected on the next occasion, and the same process repeated. It is seldom advisable to repeat the operation oftener than once in two days, except in cases of great urgency, and when the urethra is irritable, only every three of four days.

By continuing in this manner, the stricture gradually yields, and a bougie, as large as the orifice will permit to enter, will at last proceed through the whole passage without meeting with an obstacle. The operation should not be wholly laid aside, but continued until the disposition for contraction is entirely removed; and the patient should occasionally examine his urethra, every month or two, lest he encounter a relapse.

SYPHILIS.

Syphilis is another and more violent form of the venereal disease than gonorrhea. It is characterized by the appearance of a pimple surrounded by a slight inflammation, and the formation of an ulcer or chancre. The ulcer generally appears in from five to fourteen days after exposure.

Chancres are of different varieties, and may be very destructive to the organ, and there is generally a bubo or swelling in the groin, which appears in a few days after the ulcer; this swelling may continue until matter forms, when it may break, or require to be opened.

When syphilis affects the constitution, it is known as secondary and tertiary; it then shows itself in the forms of eruptions, sore throat, and ulcers in different parts of the body.

The eruption generally appears on the forehead, back, legs and arms, copper colored, attended with slight itching; the pustule is sometimes filled with a pale fluid. When the mouth and throat are affected, the parts become swollen and sore, or red and covered with a white membrane, or there may be a pale yellow ulcer of the throat or tonsils, or a dark, livid, and sloughing ulcer, which may extend to the various parts about the throat, and nose, destroying the bones of the face.

Treatment.

As soon as the ulcer appears on the penis, it should be immediately touched with caustic. The caustics which may be used are Nitrate of Silver, Nitric Acid, Caustic Potass, Chloride of Zinc. The Nitrate of Silver is the most used, and the pimple should be thoroughly burned. After the sore has been cauterized, a piece of lint dipped in a solution of opium, in the proportion of one drachm of opium, to four ounces of water, should be laid upon it, and the penis enveloped in a piece of muslin and covered with oiled silk.

The following solution may be used, instead of the Opium: Sulphate of Copper, 1 grain; Water, 1 ounce. This should be applied frequently, and the parts washed twice a day with castile soap and water.

The following may be taken internally: Protiodide of Mercury, 12 grains; Conserve of Roses, 1 scruple. Divide into twelve or twenty-four pills, and take one twice a day.

The following may be used with advantage in some cases: Blue Pill, ½ drachm; Extract of Henbane, 1 scruple. Make into ten pills. Dose: one pill at night.

Or this: Corrosive Sublimate, 4 grains; Extract of Opium, 5 grains. Mix and make into twenty pills. Dose: one pill night and morning.

These preparations should not be used more than five days in succession, as there is danger of producing salivation.

If salivation is produced, use the following: Chlorinated Soda, 1 ounce; Water, 2 ounces. Mix. The mouth should be rinsed out with this several times a day, being careful not to swallow any of it.

Ricord recommends Iron to be given in the proportion of one part of the Potassio-Tartrate of Iron, to six parts of water. Two teaspoonfuls given three times a day. The same preparation should be applied to the sore. The bubo or swelling in the groin, should be treated with compression. If, however, matter forms, the sore should be opened and poulticed. In case of an eruption on the skin, or when the disease shows itself in the throat or other part of the body,

Iodide of Potassium may be given as follows: Compound Infusion of Sarsaparilla, 1 pint; Iodide of Potassium, 1 ½ ounce. Mix. Dose: a teaspoonful after every meal.

The preparation called Donovan's Solution, may be

given internally, in doses of from three to five drops.

The diet should be strictly regular, the patient not being allowed to eat any stimulating food, or drink liquors.

CHAPTER XV
Self-Abuse, Nocturnal Emissions,
Impotence, Sterility

Few are aware of the extent to which self-pollution is practiced by the young of both sexes in civilized society, and none but those whose position or professional confidence brings them into advisory and intimate relations with the victims of unnatural indulgences or venereal diseases can have an adequate conception of the evils resulting therefrom. None but the medical man can trace the deplorable consequences to feeble, malformed, puny, and imperfectly organized offspring, and no one but the physiologist can clearly see all the external marks of exhausted vitality and premature decay stamped indelibly on thousands of our young men and maidens otherwise in the bloom of youth, health and beauty.

We might fill a volume with instances of the effects of this baneful habit, and a mere enumeration of the diseases directly or indirectly induced by these practices would occupy a far larger space than can be allowed. We shall, therefore, simply show the direct effects of the habit, and give plain and specific direction for the cure.

The abuse of amativeness rapidly exhausts the nervous power, the generative function, and takes strength from the organic and animal powers. If it fail all fail. The stomach cannot digest for want of the nervous energy spent in oft repeated and fruitless orgasms. Nutrition cannot be carried on in the capillary system. The waste matter, which should be carried off by the secreting and excreting organs, is retained to poison the foundation of life. The skin becomes dry and withered, the eye dull, the mind weak and disordered, all noble passions lose their force, the whole system is in discord and disorder, and ready to become a prey to disease. Then comes epilepsy, spinal disease, dropsy, or some form of consumption.

The genital organs are, as it were, woven into the same grand web of organic life with the stomach, heart, lungs, etc., by being largely supplied with the same class of nerves on which the organs of nutrition depend for their functional power; but the genital organs are also supplied with nerves of animal life, or those which are connected to the brain and spinal marrow. Hence the influences of the brain may act directly on the genital organs; and of these latter, on the brain. Lascivious thoughts and imaginations will excite and stimulate the genital organs, cause an increased quantity of blood to flow into them, and augment their secretions and peculiar sensibilities; and, on the other hand, the excited state of the genital organs, either from the stimulations of semen or from diseased action in the system, will throw its influence upon the brain, and force lascivious thoughts and imaginations upon the mind.

It is supposed by many that the mischief of this practice is from loss of semen. The loss of this secretion is certainly exhausting, but it is far from being the greatest evil. Boys secrete no semen before puberty, and girls never secrete any. The real source of mischief is the nervous orgasm that vivid, ecstatic, and, in its natural exercise, most delightful of sensuous enjoyments. The orgasm is almost a spasm, when prematurely excited, and though then imperfect it gives a shock to the whole system, and when often repeated the nervous power is completely exhausted. All the vitality of the body goes to supply the immature and exhausted amative organism through brain and body.

The following are given by reputable medical writers as some of the effects of this baneful habit:

Loss of memory and mental power; entire concentration of imagination on one feeling or act; a besotted, embarrassed, melancholy, and stupid look; loss of presence of mind; incapability of bearing the gaze of any one; tremors and apprehensions of future misery; morbid appetite; indigestion, and the whole train of dyspeptic symptoms; constipation; foetid breath, etc.; pale, sallow, cadaverous, or greasy-looking skin; eruptions over the face; hollowness, and lack of lustre in the eyes, with a dark circle around them; feebleness of the whole body; indisposition to make any exertion; weakness, weariness, and dull pain in the small of the back; creeping sensation in the spine; finally there comes insanity or idiocy or atrophy and death by consumption.

Self-pollution is the most certain, though not always the most immediate and direct avenue to destruction. It constitutes a lingering species of mortality, and if it were possible to study and invent refinements in cruelty, surely that would most clearly deserve the designation, which a man points deliberately against himself, against not merely his temporal but eternal welfare; not by sudden wrench to tear himself away from the amenities of wife, children, and home, but with his own hand imperceptibly to infuse a deadly poison, slowly to rankle in the cup of life and embitter each passing day; to shroud in gloom the darkening future, and invite the king of terrors prematurely to do his office.

A youth endowed by Nature with talent and genius becomes dull or totally stupid; the mind loses all relish for virtuous and exalted ideas; the consciousness of the purity and essential holiness of the Creator, operates as a bar against any approach to him or the appropriation of any of those consolations under suffering which religion is destined to afford.

All his fire and spirit are deadened by this detestible vice; he is like a faded rose, a tree blasted in its bloom, a wandering skeleton; nothing remains but debility, languor, livid paleness, a withered body, and a degraded soul. The whole life of such a man is a continued succession of secret reproach, painful sensations, arising from the consciousness of having been the fabricator of his own distress, irresolution, disgust of life, and not unfrequently self-murder. Nay, what in effect is this but the consummation of slow self-destruction? Could we but lift the veil of the grave, how should we startle at the long train of the victims of sensualism.

The first step to be taken for the cure of these sad effects is at once and forever abandon the filthy habit. There must be no indecision here, no temporizing it must be broken off at once, and then by attention to a strict hygienic regimen a cure will be effected.

The only power on earth by which the diseased and disordered body can possibly regain health is by Nature's own renovating process, which sometimes seems to work slowly, and for a long time to make no progress. If the system is very much reduced and the patient afflicted with involuntary nocturnal emissions, and distressed with pains and impaired senses, and enfeebled mind, and cheerless melancholy, tending to despair and madness, he must remember the general and special sympathies and reciprocities which exist between the genital organs and the alimentary canal and the brain; and remember, too, that in this morbid and exceedingly excitable and irritable condition of the system, things which may seem too trifling to deserve notice may nevertheless, be sufficient to keep up the disorders of the body, and therefore it is hardly possible to be too cautious, while in this condition, in the regard to everything which concerns regimen and conduct. Every irritation, every undue excitement of the brain, stomach and intestines, is calculated to continue the involuntary emissions, while the latter, in turn, keep up and increase the morbid irritability of those organs. Improper quantities of the best aliment in nature will produce the same effect; and so also will the presence of food in the stomach, duodenum, etc., at improper times. An over-full intestine or a late supper, will almost invariably cause this evil in those who are liable to such an affliction; and while those emissions continue, it is impossible for the system to recover strength and health. Costiveness of the bowels is also sure to keep up the nightly discharges; and if recourse be had to medicine, for the purpose of keeping the bowels open, it is sure to perpetuate the mischief, by irritating and debilitating still more the tissues of the alimentary canal, and, through them, the whole system.

The food, therefore, must be of such a character as will pass through the stomach and intestines with the least irritation and oppression, while it at the same time affords sufficient nourishment, and causes a free and healthy action of the bowels. Farinaceous food, properly prepared, is incomparably the best aliment, and good bread, made of coarsely ground, unbolted wheat, rye, or Indian corn, is also admitted to be one of the very best articles of diet that can be used.

When the nightly emissions are frequent, and the system very much irritated, the patient should confine himself to a few articles of diet, and eat but little, carefully avoiding full and late suppers. No animal food should be used at all, and no other drink but pure water should be ever drunk.

Many young men, by observing these rules, have been entirely relieved from emissions, but on drinking a single glass of wine, brandy-and-water, or malt liquors, or a cup of coffee, or eating a full meal, it would cause the emissions to come on again the succeeding night. The patient cannot be too careful to observe a strict undeviating regimen, and to scrupulously avoid spirits, wine, malt liquors, and every kind of alcoholic drink, even in the smallest quantity; and opium, tobacco, coffee, tea, and all other narcotics; and pepper, ginger, mustard, horse-radish, peppermint, and, in short, every stimulating and heating substance.

If the patient requires something more warming and stimulating than farinaceous food and water, to increase the tone and action of the organs, and enable them to perform their functions satisfactorily, he should not use stimulants, which, while they increase the action, necessarily deteriorate the functional results, and impair the vital properties of the tissues on which they act, especially when there are natural, healthy and invigorating means of increasing the tone and action of his organs, and general vigor of his system by active exercise. Let him exhilarate himself by copious draughts of the pure air of heaven. Let him go to the gymnasium and with moderate beginning, and moderate increase of effort, let him swing upon and climb poles, the ropes and ladders, and vault upon the wooden horse and practice all the other feats of that admirable institution; or let him walk and jump and run, or labor on the farm; and avoid sedentary habits and all anxieties and excitements of the mind; and most strictly shun all dalliance with females, and all lewd books, and obscene conversation and lascivious images and thoughts. Let him sleep on a hard bed, and rise early in the morning and take a shower bath of cold water, or plunge into cold water, or sponge his body all over with it; and, in either case, rub himself off briskly and freely with a good stiff flesh-brush; and then exercise vigorously in the open air, or in the gymnasium, for an hour before breakfast. Let him exercise as much as he can through the day, let him take an early, light supper, and take a good deal of active exercise before going to bed; and if his nocturnal emissions still continue, let him just before going to bed, repeat his shower or sponge or sitz-bath, and follow it freely with the coarse towel.

Let him perseveringly observe this regimen, without the slightest deviation in a single instance, and let him increase his exercise with his increasing strength avoiding constantly an excess of aliment; and after a while his nocturnal emissions and other disorders will disappear and his strength and general vigor will increase and he will become cheerful and sprightly, and feel as if new life and new hopes were dawning on him; and when he is fully established in these improvements, he may gradually relax the rigor of his diet, and take a greater variety of simple vegetables and fruits; but still he had better never go beyond the vegetable kingdom and pure water for his aliment.

By these means if by any, short of miraculous power, and by these alone, can the unhappy sufferer hope to be restored to comfortable and permanent health and enjoyment. The progress will be slow, but incomparably the safest and surest; and health restored in this way will put his body in a condition which will, in the greatest degree, secure it from future prostration and suffering, and from transmitting the evils of his former errors to an innocent and helpless progeny.

Seminal Emissions.

There are few diseases whose victims are in a more pitiable condition than those who suffer from seminal losses. Very many cases have come under our observation, and the following advice, when faithfully followed, has been attended with benefit.

The general trouble loss of semen and consequent exhaustion, takes place under several different circumstances. In some cases, the seminal loss is attended by a voluptuous dream. Such dreams occur to passionate persons of both sexes. Where this action occurs but seldom, and in consequence of the accumulation of vital power in this part of the organism, it cannot be a source of any great mischief, though a poor substitute for the natural gratification of amative desire, but in men, in certain states of the system there comes on an excessive excitability or irritability of the organs, which makes these dreams occur with exhausting frequency. The semen is continually voided, with a ruinous expenditure of nervous power. The seminal vesicles are irritated by the presence of the smallest quantity of the fluid; the nervous action is excited, and the exhaustion follows. It is difficult for any well man to conceive of the weak, hopeless, miserable, despairing condition of the victim of this disease. He feels coming upon him all the consequences of masturbation, without having the power to prevent them. The habit is not within his volition. The nervous organism is performing for itself what the voluntary muscles perform for the victim of solitary vice. Hundreds of young men are given to suicide by this disease hundreds more drown the sense of suffering by the excesses of dissipation. All hope of genial life is destroyed. There is no love, no marriage, no children, no ambition for all the power of body and mind is wasted. In some cases, the action seems confined to the spinal center, the cerebellum no longer acts. The semen is voided unconsciously. Sometimes, in extreme cases, it oozes away without erection, or the slightest sensation of pleasure, even passing off with the urine.

Masturbation is the cause of this terrible disease, in nine cases in ten. When the victim of this diseased habit would stop, he finds that a fiend has taken the place of his volition; a fiend he has raised but cannot quell. Continence is sometimes supposed to be the cause, such cases however, are extremely doubtful. All diseasing and debilitating influence may cooperate in causing this condition. Exhaustion, even by natural means, especially in promiscuous or unloving unions, may bring on the irritability or weakness. Married men have it occasionally as well as single. There is no more potent cause than tobacco; and the whole class of nervous stimulants favor this action. It is only a particular direction of what we call nervousness.

The weakness may also result from worms in the rectum. It may be known by an itching near the base of the penis. These may readily be removed by injections of warm water. As much water should be thrown up as the rectum will hold, and this must be allowed to descend suddenly, when it will wash out whatever worms may be within reach of the water.

In regard to the cure, there are but two or three directions to be given, beside those already given for the cure of masturbation. Let the patient, in all respects, as far as possible, place himself in the conditions of health. Let him regulate his food by his digestion, carefully evacuate his bowels every night, sleep cool, and before going to bed, take a sitz-bath, beginning at a temperature of ninety degrees. Day after day cool gradually, at the rate of one degree a day. In this way you will moderate the action of the parts, and allay irritability. Cold water may be applied night and morning to the cerebellum. In the morning take a full bath of cold water, and a thorough rubbing. As the cure progresses, the patient will have his sitz-baths colder, and may apply other means of invigoration, as dashing cold water upon the genitals, the rising douche, etc.

Use also the following tonic: Rose water, 6 ounces; Syrup of Orange Peel, 1 ounce; Muriated Tincture of Iron, 1 ounce. Mix. Dose, one teaspoonful in a wine glass of water after each meal.

Several appliances are sold for the purpose of stopping these emissions; they are generally a ring, modified more or less, that is placed on the penis when in a quiet state, so that its erection and enlargement cannot take place without awaking the patient from the pressure of the ring. These contrivances are to be avoided. They cannot do good, and may cause much injury to the urethra and seminal ducts.

By persistently following this treatment, a cure is certain. In most cases no medicines of any kind are required and the cure is in the patient's own hands. Strict attention to the laws of health, morally and physically, is all that is necessary to effect a complete and permanent cure. Sufferers from this infirmity are generally too anxious about symptoms, they are continually watching and fretting about the urine, urinary pains, etc., and an excited and nervous imagination magnifies ordinary trifles into serious and alarming indications. The best plan is to pay no attention to these matters whatever. If any symptom is very alarming, application to the family physician or any respectable practitioner would set matters right. Marriage has been recommended as a cure for seminal weakness, but it more frequently aggravates and increases the disease. Before the marriage relation is entered into, the health should be fully restored.

Impotence and Sterility.

Impotence is an absolute cause of sterility, because it prevents the conditions necessary to fecundation from taking place; but although the act of coitus may be accomplished, it does not follow that the person should always be able to perpetuate his species. Stricture of the urethra may prevent the discharge of seminal fluid; or the fluid may be directed toward the bladder or the parietes of the urethra, by deviation of the orifices of the ejaculatory ducts. The secretion may be altered in its nature, it may only contain imperfect spermatozoa, etc. A man may, therefore, be unfruitful without being impotent.

Masturbation leads directly to impotence in men and women, and often to sterility in the former. Barrenness is women is not as in men, the result of impotence. The organs, external and internal, may lose their sensibility to pleasure and still the ovaries may form their germs and the uterus may nourish them. Barrenness in women may proceed from galling or other displacement of the womb; from the closing of its mouth; from leucorrhoea or whites, or other diseased discharge, which may arrest and destroy the zoospermes; or it may be caused by inflammation, or excessive irritability of the uterus by which the embryos are thrown off in a series of early abortions, and the same result may be produced by the frequent excitement of amativeness.

The cure of sterility in men in those rare cases in which it exists without impotence, must come with health. Use the same treatment as for masturbation.

The cure for impotence must be a course of gradual invigoration. Put the patient into the best of possible healthy conditions, and the cure will come.

135

In addition to these means, the following may be taken: Hoxham's Tincture of Cinchona, 4 ounces; Diluted Phosphoric Acid, ½ ounce; Tincture of Nux Vomica, 2 drachms. Mix. Dose, 1 teaspoonful every 3 hours.

The impotence of women requires corresponding treatment, with bathing, the sitz-bath, the wet bandage and the vagina syringe.

Take also the following pills: Citrate of Iron, 1 drachm; Sulphate of Quinine, 1 scruple; Extract of Nux Vomica, 8 grains. Mix. Make into 32 pills. Dose, 1 pill three times a day.

But when barrenness comes from excessive action, it must be treated like nymphomania.

Nymphomania in women, and Satyriasis in men, are the names given to inflamed and excited conditions of the generative function. The seats of this disease are in the cerebellum, extending to the whole brain and involving every feeling; the lower part of the spinal cord, exiting continual erections and automatic and spasmodic action in the generative organs.

Its causes are masturbation; exciting diet; an indolent, sensual and voluptuous life, and continence, or forced abstinence from the enjoyments of love.

The symptoms of this disease are an excessive and perpetual desire for sexual intercourse, a mind filled with lascivious ideas, excited to frenzy by every voluptuous image. There is no longer any discrimination of beauty, fitness or attraction; to the diseased man every female, and even a female animal, is an object of desire. Under its influence men have committed rapes on little children and aged women, and committed other vile abominations.

When women and girls are effected with nymphomania, there are similar and even more striking manifestations.

When the disease is brought on by masturbation, the habit must of course be at once broken off and some active occupation be engaged to absorb the whole energies of body and mind.

A spare and entirely unstimulating diet, the sitz-bath, the cold douche, or ice-water to the cerebellum, are plainly indicated. The vagina syringe helps to overcome the inflammation of the womb, and the wet bandage, often renewed, should be worn around the loins by women, and should cover the genital organs in men. The treatment is, in fact, very similar to that for masturbation, or inflammation of any other part of the system.

CHAPTER XVI
Diseases Peculiar to Women.
Delayed and Obstructed Menstruation.

When the menses do not appear at the time when they may naturally be expected, we call it delayed or obstructed menstruation. It is, however, of great importance to know whether a girl is sufficiently developed to make it necessary for the menses to appear, although she may have reached the proper age. As long as the girl has not increased physically, if she has not become wider across the hips, if her breasts have not become enlarged, and if she experiences none of the changes incident to this period, an effort to force nature is positively injurious. In this case a general treatment will be called for. She should be required to exercise freely in the open air, retire early to bed, and arise at an early hour in the morning. She should not be allowed to be closely confined at school, if attending. Her diet should be generous, but free from all rich food, which will disorder the stomach. If, however, she is fully developed, and she suffers from time to time from congestion of the head, breast, or abdomen, it will be necessary to interfere. The following are the symptoms which will generally be found in these cases: Headache, weight, fullness, and throbbing in the centre of the cranium, and in the back part of the head; pains in the back and loins; cold feet and hands. becoming sometimes very hot; skin harsh and dry; slow pulse, and not unfrequently attended with epilepsy.

Treatment: It is well for the patient, a few days before the period, to take a warm hip or foot bath twice a day, and at night when retiring to apply cloths wet in warm water to the abdomen.

The bowels should be kept open, by some mild cathartic as castor oil, or a pill of Aloes.

If there is pain and fullness of the head during the discharge, or before it, use the following: Tincture of Aconite leaves, 2 drachms; Tincture of Belladonna, 1 drachm; Tincture of Cantharides, 1 drachm; Morphia, 3 grains; Simple Syrup, 4 ounces. Dose: one teaspoonful three times a day. If the pain is severe it may be taken every two hours.

Between the periods, if the system is weak, the following may be taken: Precip. Carbonate of Iron, 5 drachms; Extract Conium, 2 drachms; Balsam Peru, 1 drachm; Alcohol, 4 ounces; Oil of Wintergreen, 20 drops; Simple Syrup, 8 ounces. Dose: two teaspoonfuls three times a day. Shake the mixture before using.

Chlorosis or Green Sickness.

This disease generally occurs in young unmarried females, who are weak and delicate. It manifests itself about the age of puberty, and is accompanied by feeble appetite, and digestion. There is no menstrual discharge, or else it is very slight.

It is caused by unnutritious food, residence in damp and unventilated apartments. It may be hereditary, all the females in the family being liable to the same disease. Those who drink largely of tea, coffee, diluted acids, bad wines, and indulge in tight lacing, are predisposed to this disease. Among the exciting causes may be mentioned disturbing emotions, unrequited love, home sickness, depression of spirits, &c.

If we take into consideration the fact that the cause of the disease is impoverishment of the blood, the treatment will not be difficult. Exercise freely in the open air; protect the body from chilliness by warm clothing, and plenty of it. The patient should sleep on a mattress in a well ventilated room. The diet should be nourishing, without being stimulating. It is important that the habits should be regular, and the mind kept cheerful by society and innocent amusements. Before the medical treatment is commenced, the exciting causes of the disease must be removed. A complete change must be made in the existence of the patient. If she is confined closely at school, she must be removed; if she is inclined to confine herself to the home, send her to the country. Picture to her the danger she is in, by the continuance of such a life; give her plenty of outdoor exercise. The mental and moral causes are the most difficult to remove, but a change in scenery and new friends will do much towards it. For those who are shut up in factories, or who work all day in a stooping position, a change of employment must be made. A bath of tepid water in the morning followed by brisk rubbing will be beneficial. Also the frequent use of the sitting bath, and the sponge bath in the evening. Active exercise should precede and follow all baths. During menstruation all applications of water should be omitted.

The following recipes are recommended by Dr. Pancoast, of Philadelphia. They are to be taken on alternate days; that is, take No. 1 on one day, No. 2 the next day, and so on.

No. 1: Precip. Carbonate of Iron, 5 drachms; Extract of Conium, 2 drachms; Balsam Peru, 1 drachm; Oil Cinnamon, 20 drops; Simple Syrup, 8 ounces; Pulverized Gum Arabic, 2 drachms. Mix. Dose: two teaspoonfuls three times a day, every other day, after meals. Shake before using.

No. 2: Tincture of Nux Vomica, 1 drachm; Syrup Iodide of Iron, 1 ounce; Simple Syrup, 4 ounces. Mix. Dose: one teaspoonful three times every other day, in water after meals.

Another treatment is as follows. Clear the bowels with the following mixture: Sulphate of Magnesia, 1 ounce; Nitrate of Potash, 10 grains; Extract of Licorice, 1 scruple; Compound Infusion of Senna, 5 ½ ounces; Tincture of Jalap, 3 drachms; Spirit of Sal Volatile, 1 drachm. Mix. Dose: two or three tablespoonfuls at a time, at intervals of two hours, until an effect is produced.

This is to be followed by Sulphate of Iron, 5 grains; Extract of Gentian, 10 grains. Make into three pills, and take a pill twice a day, with the Compound of aloes or Rhubarb pill every night.

Profuse Menstruation Menorrhagia.

By Menorrhagia we understand an immoderate flow of the menses. There is no fixed amount of blood which is lost at the menstrual period, but it varies in different women. It will average, however, from four to eight ounces. The quantity discharged may be estimated by the number of napkins used. Each napkin will contain half an ounce, or one tablespoonful, so that eight napkins should contain four ounces; twenty ten ounces, etc. In some females the discharge will be excessive without impairment of the general health.

Some females are disposed to uterine hemorrhages, from a relaxed or flabby state of the uterus. Frequent child-bearing, abortion, high living, too prolonged and frequent suckling, may induce flooding. Among the exciting causes we may mention, over-exertion, dancing, falls, lifting heavy weights, cold, and mental excitement.

Treatment: The patient must lie down on a hard bed, and abstain from all stimulating food and drinks. The room should be cool, and she should be lightly covered with bed clothes. Soak the feet in warm water, and if the flowing is excessive apply cloths, wrung out in vinegar and water, to the lower bowels. The hips must be elevated higher than the head. Only in extreme cases should plugging be resorted to. This may be done by pieces of linen, about four inches square, thrust into the vagina, until it is full, and a bandage applied between the legs. Cold hip baths, and vaginal injections will be beneficial when the hemorrhage is slight.

Use also the following: Diluted Sulphuric Acid, 2 drachms; Syrup of Orange Peel, 2 ounces; Cinnamon Water, one ounce. Mix. Dose: a teaspoonful in a wineglass of water, two or three times a day.

If there is much pain administer the following every two or three hours: Morphia, 1/4 grain; Cayenne, 4 grains; Rosin, 4 grains; Mix. Give in Blackberry Syrup.

Painful Menstruation Menstrual Colic
Dysmenorrhea

The word dysmenorrhea means a difficult monthly flow, and is always preceded by severe pains in the back and lower part of the abdomen. It is caused by taking cold during the period; fright, violent mental emotions; obstinate constipation; sedentary occupations; smallness of the mouth and neck of the womb. Females subject to this trouble are generally relieved by marriage. The symptoms are severe bearing down pains in the region of the uterus like labor pains; restlessness, coldness, flashes of heat, with headache; aching in the small of the back, lower part of the abdomen, and thighs; the discharge is scanty, and contains shreds of fiber and clotted blood.

Treatment: The patient should immediately go to bed, and cover up warmly. Stimulating food and drinks should be avoided. Use a warm foot bath and sitting bath, with hot poultices of hops, or cloths, wet in hot water applied to the abdomen.

In the interval of the menses, take active exercise, with a tepid hip bath, three nights in the week, injecting some water high into the vagina. Keep the bowels open with a pill of Aloes and Myrrh, and take a small teaspoonful of the volatile Tincture of Guaiacum, three times a day in water.

On the approach of the period, take the following at night: Calomel, 3 grains; Opium, 1 grain. In the morning, a dose of Castor Oil, and on the appearance of the menses, the Dover's Powder and a mixture as before. Repeat this treatment in each interval, until permanently relieved.

The following is recommended by Prof. Meigs, to be taken a few days before the period: Acetous Tincture of Colchicum, 3 drachms; Magnesia, 1 drachm; Sulphate of magnesia, 3 drachms; Distilled Mint, or Cinnamon Water, 4 ounces. Mix. Dose: a small wine-glassful every two or three hours, until it operates. This should be preceded, the night before, by a small dose of blue pill.

Suppression of the Menses (Amenorrhea)

By suppression is meant a disappearances of the menses, after they have become established; this may be either acute or chronic. It is caused by cold, caught during the flow, by exposure to night air, or by wetting the feet, fear, shocks, violent mental emotions, anxiety, fevers, and other acute diseases. Chronic suppression may be either a consequence of the acute, or caused by delicate health; also from diseases of the ovaries, or womb. It may also be occasioned by an imperforate hymen, in which case it must be cut open by a physician.

When the suppression is caused by some disease in the

system, that disease must be cured before the menses will return. For sudden suppression, use the warm sitting bath or foot bath. Apply cloths wet in warm water to the lower part of the abdomen, and drink freely of warm water. If the suppression is chronic, and the patient is delicate, in the interval between the menses, use the shower, or the full bath of cold or tepid water, rubbing the body briskly with a coarse towel, especially around the abdomen, loins, and genital organs.

As soon as the discharge has ceased, a warm hip bath will generally bring it on.

If there is much inflammation of the uterus give the following: Tincture Aconite leaves, 2 drachms; Sweet Spirit of Nitre, 1 ounce; Simple Syrup, 8 ounces. Dose: one teaspoonful every two or three hours.

If the discharge cannot be brought on, wait until the next period. A few day before the term, the bowels should be freely opened, and kept open until the period for the discharge has arrived. The pill of Aloes and Iron of the United States Dispensatory, is one of the best that can be given. Give from one to three pills daily.

If there is no evident reason for the discharge not appearing, such as pregnancy, inflammation of the neck of the womb, and the woman is suffering from the suppression, use the following: Caulophyllin, 1 drachm; Extract Aconite, 8 grains; Aloes, 10 grains; Sulphate of Iron, 10 grains. Make into 40 pills. Dose: two or three pills taken night and morning.

The remedies should always be taken a few days before the period arrives for the menses. If chronic suppression is the result of any acute disease, the health must first be re-established, otherwise it would be wrong to force the menses. When this has been done, immediately before the return of the period, a warm hip bath should be taken every night for six nights.

One of the following pills taken three times a day: Fresh powdered Ergot of Rye, 50 grains; Barbadoes Aloes, 12 grains; Essential Oil of Juniper, 12 drops. Make into twelve pills, with syrup or mucilage, washing down each pill with a cup of Pennyroyal tea.

Cessation of the Menses Change of Life.

By the phrase "change of life," or the critical period, we understand the final cessation, or stoppage of the menses. It usually takes place between the ages of forty and fifty, although in some cases it may occur as early as thirty, and in others not until sixty; however, we can expect the change about the forty-fifth year.

The symptoms will vary according to the constitution of the woman; in some the change occurs by the discharge gradually diminishing in quantity, in others by the intervals between the periods being lengthened. The woman may pass this period, without having any more unpleasant symptoms than an occasional rush of blood to the head, or a headache. Others, however, may have very severe symptoms arise, which will require the care of an intelligent physician. These disagreeable sensations should receive careful consideration, and not be hushed up with the reply, that these complaints arise from "the change of life," and will vanish whenever that change takes place. The foundation of serious trouble may be laid, which will make the remainder of her existence a burden, and cut short a life which might have been conducted to a great old age. While this change is in progress, in probably the majority of cases, there is more or less disturbance of the health. It is sometimes quite impossible to say exactly what is the trouble with the patient, except that she is out of health. The following are some of the symptoms which may arise: Headache, dizziness, biliousness, sour stomach, indigestion, diarrhea, costiveness, piles, itching of the private parts; cramps and colic in the bowels; palpitation of the heart; swelling of the limbs and abdomen; pains in the back and loins; paleness and general weakness.

Treatment: Eat and drink moderately; sleep in airy, well ventilated rooms; avoid stimulants; exercise daily in the open air, either by walking or riding; avoid violent emotions; shun exposure to wet, stormy weather, wet feet, etc.

Keep the bowels regulated with the following: Mercurial Pill, 1 grain; Ipecac Powder, ½ grain; Compound Rhubarb Pill, 3 grains. Mix; a pill to be taken every night.

Or: one ounce of Hicra Picra, or powdered Aloes with Castella, mixed with a pint of gin, which should stand for four or five days, after which a tablespoonful in a glass of water may be taken every morning, or second morning as the case may be.

If the patient is large and fleshy, of full habit, the following is recommended: Sulphate of Magnesia, 1½ ounces; Compound Infusion of Roses, 5 ounces; Cinnamon Water, 1 ounce. Mix. Dose: two tablespoonfuls twice a day.

If there are nervous symptoms prominent, give: Valerianate of Zinc, 8 grains; Tincture of Valerian, 2 drachms; Orange Flower Water, 3½ ounces; Syrup of Red Poppies, 2 drachms. Mix. Dose: a tablespoonful every six hours.

Falling of the Womb (Prolapsis Uteri)

Falling of the womb is simply a sinking down of the organ, and may be so slight as not to be noticed, or so great that the organ will protrude between the legs through the external opening. It is not a disease of the womb itself, but of some of its supports.

So long as the vagina retains its natural size, and the ligaments are but two and a half inches long, the organ will not be displaced. Whatever tends to relax and weaken the system, may cause the complaint. The muscles of the abdomen which support the intestines being weakened from any cause, will allow the intestines to press down upon the womb and its ligaments, and, in consequence of this constant pressure, they give way. Another cause is too early exercise after child-bearing. Flooding, and leucorrhea or whites, if allowed to continue for a long time will produce it. In delicate females, continued running up and own stairs, also tight lacing, dancing, leaping, and running, particularly during the period of menstruation, when the womb is increased by the weight of blood contained in it. The use of medicines to loosen the bowels, which is very common among many, is still another cause of the disorder.

Most females who are troubled with the falling of the womb, think that it is necessary to a cure that they should wear some kind of a support to the abdomen. These supports, however, do a vast amount of harm, for by being worn tightly around the abdomen, they increase the pressure on the bowels, thus forcing down, more and more, the womb and its appendages. All that is necessary is to raise the womb to its natural position, and use an instrument that will keep it in place. This instrument is called a pessary. This pessary is a ring, or hollow, cup-shaped globe, made of gold, silver, ivory, wood or gutta percha, and is placed in the vagina, or birth place, thus supporting the womb. The cold hip bath should be used once a day, at the same time injecting cold water into the vagina, with a syringe. Lie down as much as possible, and avoid becoming fatigued. Apply cold bandages to the abdomen upon going to bed.

If the womb has descended to the external orifice, it is often necessary to restore it ot its natural position by pressing it upward and backward by a finger or two pressed into the vagina. If the process be accompanied with pain, the vagina should be well washed by injections of thick flax-seed or slippery-elm bark tea for a day or two before the astringent washes are used.

Avoid tight corsets and heavy skirts, suspend the under garments from the shoulders and not from the waist, as is usually done. Use plain vegetable diet and avoid tea, coffee, spirituous drinks and all sensual indulgences. Allow the clothes to be loose. These things must be attended to closely. The diet should be plain and nourishing, but not stimulating.

Use an injection of an infusion of White Oak Bark, Geranium, or a solution of Alum, in the proportion of one ounce to the pint of water. If there is inflammation of the womb, this must be subdued before using the pessary. Give Tincture of Aconite, compound powder of Ipecac and Opium with injections of an infusion of Hops and Lobelia, or an infusion of Belladonna.

If there is heat and difficulty in passing water, drink an infusion of Marsh mallow and Spearmint.

If the patient is weak, give the following tonic: Sulphate of Quinine, 25 grains; Citrate of Iron (soluble) 35 grains. Make into 24 powders. Take a powder three times a day, after each meal in sweet wine.

Leucorrhea, Whites, Fluor Albus.

The word leucorrhea is derived from two Greek words and means literally "white discharge." It is also known as"Fluor Albus," "Whites," and "Female Weakness," and consists of a "light colorless discharge from the genital organs, varying in hue from a whitish or colorless, to a yellowish, light green, or to a slightly red or brownish; varying in consistency from a thin watery, to a thick, tenacious, ropy substance; and in quantity from a slight increase in the healthy secretion, to several ounces, in twenty-four hours."

This discharge generally occurs between the age of fifteen and forty-five, seldom during infancy or old age. When it occurs in young female children, it will not unfrequently be produced by the presence of pin worms in the vagina, which make their way there from the rectum. There will be intense itching of the parts, and the worms can be removed with a small piece of cloth, after separating the lips.

This disease may be either acute or chronic. The acute form generally results from taking cold, and is simply a catarrhal inflammation of the mucous membrane lining the vagina. The chronic form is but a continuation of the acute, and is generally caused by the acute stage having been neglected or improperly treated. Ulceration of the neck of the womb sometimes results. There are two forms of leucorrhea: vaginal leucorrhea, when the discharge comes from the walls of the vagina; and cervical leucorrhea, when the discharge proceeds from the neck of the womb.

Causes: Taking cold from sitting on the ground, or exposure of the neck and shoulders; over sexual excitement, and sexual intercourse; tight lacing; piles; miscarriages and abortions; displacement of the womb; purgatives; improper articles of diet; warm injection, or injections of any kind; late hours, etc. It may also be hereditary.

The treatment, to be successful, requires that the patient should first be placed in a favorable condition. Anything which tends to excite the disease, must be avoided, as dissipations, late suppers, etc. The diet must be plain and nourishing without being stimulating, and be taken regularly. Exercise, short of fatigue, will be beneficial. The clothing should be warm, and worn loosely, especially about the waist. Water is of great importance in the treatment of this trouble. The sitting bath may be used every day, and injections of cold or tepid water should be used, three or four times a day, according to the severity of the discharge.

An injection of weak green tea will be found good in some mild cases, as also sweet cider, or a weak solution of alum.

One of the best tonics is the Muriated Tincture of Iron, of which take twenty or twenty-five drops in half a tumbler of water, three or four times a day. An excellent injection is made by taking three drachms of Tannic acid, and an ounce of Alum, dissolving them in a quart of water; inject one-third, three times a day. The bowels should be kept open by Rochelle or Epsom Salts or Seidlitz Powder.

Where there is great debility of the organs, or when the disease has been brought on by exposure to cold, pregnancy, abortions, etc., the following will be found very successful: Tincture of Aloes, 2 ounces; Muriated Tincture of Iron, 4 drachms. Mix. Dose: thirty-five drops in water, three times a day.

At the same time use the following injection: Sulphate of Zinc, (white Vitriol,) 2 drachms; Sugar of Lead, 2 drachms. Mix in one quart of water, and use one-fourth for each injection.

CHAPTER VII
Ready Remedies for Common Complaints.

Abscess.--A collection of matter produced by inflammation.
Treatment: Take a slightly cooling and gentle aperient. If the abscess goes on regularly, leave it undisturbed, until its pointed shape and the thinness of the skin show its fitness for lancing. Do not squeeze it. Foment the part with hot flannel, and apply a poultice of linseed-meal mixed with milk and water, or bread mixed with oil. In parts where the poultice is difficult to retain, it must be put into a bag made of muslin or lena, with a tape attached to each corner of the bag to fasten it on and retain it to its place. The poultice should be renewed every six or eight hours, and continued for some days. After discharging pretty freely, a slip of lint should be inserted by a probe, and renewed once or twice a day, according to the nature of the discharge. After this, the part should be supported by a bandage, or slips of adhesive or soap plaster to facilitate contraction; and the aperture should be left open to favor the discharge. When healed, tonic medicine and change of air, should be resorted to. During the continuance of the abscess, the patient should live on food which is plain and nutritious, without being stimulating, avoiding at the same time wine, spirits, and beer.

Acidity of the Stomach. A common symptom of weak or disordered digestion.
Treatment: Small doses of carbonate of soda, or ammonia, or sal-volatile in water three or four times a day, with some tonic bitter added. Diet, light and nutritious; take as much out-of-door exercise as possible, and keep the bowels regular by the use of some mild aperient.

Ague. Chills and fever. A species of fever, which comes on only at stated intervals. [Malaria, before cause and prevention were understood. Ed.]
Treatment: In the cold stage, give warm diluent drinks, as barley water, weak tea, or weak wine and water. Apply external warmth by means of extra clothing, hot bottles to the feet, mustard foot-baths, bags of heated bran, baked salt, &c. In this stage, an opiate

149

if often beneficial; give twenty-five to fifty drops of laudanum, with an equal quantity of ether, in a glass of water. During the hot stage, an opposite mode of treatment must be adopted. Sponge the surface with tepid or cold water, give gold diluent or iced drinks, and administer a full dose of laudanum. When the hot stage has subsided into the sweating stage, the action of the skin should be encouraged by tepid drinks; and if the system is much exhausted, weak spirit and water in small quantities may be occasionally ventured on. During intermissions, administer active aperients, as five grains of calomel, with three grains of compound extract of colocynth, followed by a mild purgative. Give bark [quinine, ED.] to an extent as great as the stomach will bear and combine with it wine and aromatics, accompanied by a generous but light diet, and moderate exercise.

Treatment: Quinine is a very powerful agent in ague; two or three grains of this medicine, administered twice or thrice daily, with such nourishing diet as the patient can take, will in ordinary cases, put a speedy end to the disease.

Treatment: In cases of long standing, which resist the usual modes of treatment, the following remedy may be had recourse to: Iodide of potassium, one and a half drachms; peppermint water, twelve ounces; take two tablespoonfuls every four hours. One or two grains of sulphate of quinine may be added to each dose.

Treatment: Agues are liable to return, and persons subject to the complaint are always made aware of its approach. In such cases, the fit may be rendered milder by taking one scruple of ipecacuhana in an ounce of water as an emetic, an hour previously. Sick persons should also take occasional doses of sulphate of quinine twice a day for three or four weeks; in spring and autumn, especially, night air must be avoided, and the early morning air not attempted, until some warm fluid or food has been introduced into the stomach.

Apoplexy. A sudden suspension of the mental and physical powers.

Treatment: Remove the patient to a cool, well ventilated room; place him in a reclining or sitting posture, with the head and shoulders slightly raised. Loosen all the tight parts of the sufferer's dress, especially anything pressing around the neck. Pour cold water over the head, and keep it cool by means of powdered ice in a bladder. Apply mustard plaster to the soles of the feet and the calves of the legs. If the patient be of a full habit, a dozen leeches may be applied behind the ears and on the temples. If food has been taken recently, an emetic of mustard and water may be given; and in order to promote the action of the bowels, a drop of croton oil should be placed on the tongue and repeated every two or three hours, till the end is accomplished. In persons of spare habit, a small quantity of stimulant, as wine or brandy, or a teaspoonful of sal-volatile in water, may be given every twenty minutes or half-hour. Bleeding should only be resorted to in the last extremity, where there is great danger, and the arrival of the medical man is delayed. Persons of an apoplectic temperament should live moderately, eat plain and nourishing food and avoid wine, spirits, beer, &c. Exercise and fresh air are also of the highest importance.

Appetite, Defective. The loss of appetite may arise from a variety of causes, as the excessive use of wines and spirits, the partaking immoderately of warm fluids, sedentary occupation, over-anxiety, excess of mental labor, impure air, &c.

Treatment: Regulation of diet and change of air will be frequently found more beneficial than medicine. But to restore the tone of the stomach, which is the chief aim, the following decoction may be taken: Peruvian bark, six drachms; cascarilla bark, two drachms. Bruise them in a mortar, and boil them in a pint and a half of water for a few minutes; strain off the liquor while hot, then add tincture of bark, two ounces; diluted nitric acid, one and a half drachms. Four tablespoonfuls to be taken thrice daily. Bitter tonics are also advantageous. Rhubarb chewed one hour before dinner-time is also advantageous. One or two four-grain compound aloe pills may be taken at noon with beneficial effect.

Asthma. An affection of the respiratory organs, which betrays itself in labored and anxious breathing, accompanied by a sense of suffocation and constriction of the chest.

Treatment: Place the patient in an upright position and loosen the dress, to accelerate the freedom of the action of the chest. Let him inhale decoction of stramonium, ether, or hops from the spout of a teapot. Rigid abstinence will often render the most asthmatic person comparatively free from attack. The bowels must be kept active, and the simplest diet enjoined. It is also of importance that asthmatic subjects reside in high situations, and also that they occupy the upper rooms of a house.

Another treatment: Soak blotting paper in a strong solution of saltpeter; dry it; take a piece about the size of the palm of the hand, and on going to bed, light it, and lay it upon the dressing table in the bedroom. By doing so, persons however badly affected with asthma will be able to sleep almost as well as when in health.

Back, Pains in. Pains in the back are of many kinds, and may result from a variety of causes.

Treatment: If weakness be the cause, cold bathing, the shower bath, and squeezing a sponge repeatedly down the back, together with vigorous rubbing with a rough towel, will be found efficacious. Rest, in a recumbent or semi-recumbent position, will also alleviate the pain and contribute to its removal. See Kidneys, Lumbago, Spinal Weakness, &c.

Baldness. This is caused by the disorganization of the root or bulb of the hair, and may proceed from age, general derangement of the functions, or local disease. When baldness proceeds from age, the hair can never be restored; but when arising from other causes, it may be.

Treatment: Mix well together liquor of ammonia, one ounce; camphorated alcohol, one and a half drachms; bay-salt, half ounce; water, one pint; with this mixture bathe the head three times a day. Afterwards, rub well into the scalp a pomatum made of fresh hog's lard, three and a quarter ounces, and grated camphor, one ounce. The action of the sedative water restores the capillary circulation which forms the bulb of the hair, and imparts new life to the organ. The pomatum assists and favors the growth.

Another Treatment: Castor oil, one and a half ounces; tincture of cantharides, half an ounce; mix well together, and rub the bald part with it night and morning.

Biliousness. There is scarcely a person that is not subject more or less to this complaint. It arises from a disordered state of the liver, and is most frequently brought about by over-indulgence in eating and drinking, or by partaking of unwholesome food. An excess of fat or oily matter, rich soups and gravies, pork, and highly seasoned meats, pastry, and a variety of other articles of food, too numerous to mention, are apt to generate an excess of bile. A little experience soon teaches a person "what to eat, drink, and avoid," and if he oversteps the bounds of discretion, he must of course expect to pay the penalty. But biliousness may be induced by other causes than excess in diet. A want of sufficient exercise is one of them, impure air is another, and inattention to the skin is a third. In order to ward off this excess of bile, every person ought to take two or three hours' active exercise in the open air daily. In addition to this he should either bathe in cold or tepid water every morning, or sponge the whole surface of the body, rubbing the skin afterwards with a rough towel until a comfortable warmth and healthy glow are produced. Some persons are so predisposed to biliousness, that, despite every care and precaution, they are unable to keep free from this complaint and they are compelled to have frequent recourse to medicine to keep the liver in working order.

Treatment: Compound extract of colocynth, four scruples; scammony, one scruple; extract of rhubarb, twelve grains; soap, six grains; oil of cinnamon, four drops; mix and divide into twenty-four pills. Take two at bedtime, and repeat as required.

Bladder, Irritation of.

Treatment: In ordinary cases this may be relieved by warm fomentations applied to the affected part, or by warm bathing. It is also well to avoid undue exertion, to rest in a recumbent position as much as possible, to keep the bowels well open, and to abstain from eating and drinking such things as are of a heating and stimulating nature. When the complaint assumes a more severe form, medical advice should be sought without delay.

Bleary Eye. A term given to an inflammatory appearance of the eyelids and the corners of the eye itself.

Treatment: This minor complaint is often very obstinate, arising, as it does, from some hereditary taint, and resolving itself into a constitutional defect. When resulting from age, cold, or temporary weakness, adopt the following: Mix five grains of sulphate of zinc in two tablespoonfuls of water; wet the eye from time to time with a piece of linen rag or lint dipped in this liquid.

Bleeding at the Nose. This is common with young persons, and with such as are of full habit of body. Generally speaking, it may be regarded as an effort by which Nature seeks to relieve the overcharged system, and when it does not occur too frequently, or last too long, it is as well to allow the bleeding to go on unchecked. With weak or aged persons, however, it cannot be stopped too soon.

Treatment: The sudden application of cold by driving the blood from the surface, effects a stoppage in ordinary cases. Putting a door-key down the back, bathing the face and head with cold water, or vinegar and water, exposing the body to the cool air, and drinking iced lemonade, are among these expedients. If the bleeding is difficult to check, place the person in an upright position, put a moderate pinch of powdered alum into two tablespoonfuls of water, and with a syringe inject this up the nostrils.

Bleeding from Wounds. It is of importance to know how to proceed to stop the bleeding of a wound, as many serious and severe cases have occurred through the attendant or bystander not possessing the presence of mind or tact necessary in such an emergency.

Treatment: When a wound is situated in the limbs, and is succeeded by copious and protracted bleeding, the main thing is to prevent the wholy current of blood passing through the limb. If from the upper part of the arm, the thumb should be pressed firmly into that part of the neck behind the collarbone; this will intercept the flow of blood through the principal artery of the arm as it issues from the chest. The thumb, however, is apt to become tired and relax its pressure, and nothing can answer the purpose better than the handle of a door-key wrapped in three or four folds of linen, which can be held in its position for an indefinite length of time. If the wound be high up on the leg or thigh, the thumb should be pressed immediately below the cavity of the groin, the patient, meanwhile, lying on his back. This will have the effect of arresting the flow of blood from the great artery which supplies the limbs. When the wound is situated below the middle of the upper arm, or below the middle of the thigh, a large and strong handkerchief should be bound once or twice round the limb; a piece of stick, such as a large skewer, or a small ruler, should then be introduced between the bandage and the skin, and twisted so that it screws the handkerchief tight until the flow of blood ceases. When the bleeding stops, the screwing should cease, otherwise the parts will be bruised and injured. If the wounded part be on a bone, the bleeding can be arrested by firmly pressing the finger on the bone, or by a cork, or a hard pad. It must be understood that these proceedings are to be adopted only until such time as proper assistance arrives. In every instance a surgeon ought to be sent for instantly.

Blistered Skin. The hands and feet are most liable to become blistered; the hands from unaccustomed manual employment, and the feet from excessive walking.

Treatment: When the blister is greatly puffed up, prick it with a needle so that the watery matter may discharge itself. Afterwards bathe the part with warm water. When a long walk is about to be taken, especially in hot weather, it is a good plan to rub the feet with sweet oil, which will generally prevent blisters forming.

Blood, Spitting of. A discharge of blood, often of a frothy appearance, brought up with coughing, and preceded by a saltish taste in the mouth, difficulty of breathing, and a sense of weight and pain at the chest.

Treatment: Avoidance of exertion, heat and mental disturbance. The patient should be placed in a half-sitting posture. Cool air must be freely admitted, and if necessary, the head and body sprinkled with water. All stimulating food and drink must be discarded, and cold acidulated beverages should be given to drink. If this treatment does not arrest the spitting, give a little alum in water, and keep the bowels open with castor oil or a dose of Epsom salts. When the spitting has ceased, every means should be adopted to prevent a return, and this is most effectually accomplished by the patient taking gentle carriage exercise, keeping himself quiet, and taking occasional doses of Peruvian bark.

Blotches. Under this head are comprised those unsightly pustules and pimples which appear on the face and other parts of the body.

Treatment: As blotches arise chiefly from a disordered state of the stomach and impurity of the blood, it is of the first consequence that these important agents of the system should be properly cared for. Blotches often arise from the eating of improper food, the drinking of ardent spirits, indulgence in wine, etc., sometimes from a disordered digestion, and sometimes from the want of exercise and pure air, or inattention to the skin. Where there is a tendency to this complaint, persons cannot be too particular as regards diet and regimen. The food they take should be simple, and yet nourishing; alcoholic drinks and malt liquors should be for a time foregone; fat meats, rich soups, and pastry should be especially avoided. Meanwhile, active exercise should be taken daily, until a profuse perspiration is induced, then the whole surface of the body and the face should be thoroughly rubbed with a towel. In addition to this a tepid bath should be taken every morning, and the skin submitted to a vigorous application of the flesh-brush. As occasion requires, a mild aperient, together with a saline draught, should be taken. Thus the system will be attended to internally and externally, and by persevering in this course the skin will be ultimately brought to a healthy state. In the spring and autumn seasons, owing to the changes which the blood undergoes, blotches are apt to form on the faces of person who are otherwise ordinarily healthy. A very simple remedy is a dessert-spoonful of milk of sulphur, taken in a little milk, every morning, until the blotches disappear. Another remedy, equally simple, is to boil a handful of mint leaves in a pint of water, and take a wine-glassful of the decoction twice daily. After what has been said, we need scarcely state, that to endeavor to drive away blotches by mere external and local applications, is always hurtful, and generally ineffectual; at best the impurities are forced into the system, to reappear at some future time in a more aggravated form.

Breath, Offensive. The odor of the breath is a pretty correct index of the state of the body. When tainted, it is so not uncommonly from decayed teeth, or from a morbid secretion of the tonsils; but more frequently, in children especially, it is indicative of disordered stomach and loaded bowels.

Treatment: Rinse the mouth out two or three times a day with a weak solution of soda or chloride of lime. Or: Take half a tumbler-full of camomile tea on rising every morning.

Bronchitis. Inflammation of the bronchi, or tubes which convey the air into the lungs. Acute Bronchitis makes itself known by great tightness of the chest, difficulty of breathing, and considerable pain.

Treatment: Hot bran poultices, mustard plasters, or blisters, should be applied to the chest, throat, and between the shoulders. An emetic should be given, and repeated at the end of twenty-four hours, if the symptoms have not decreased in severity. After a while there should be administered two grains each of calomel and James's powder every six hours. The patient should be kept in bed, and the temperature of the chamber carefully equalized. The diet should be light.

Chronic Bronchitis. This form of the disease generally makes its appearance towards the end of autumn, and is seldom got rid of until the end of spring. As feebleness commonly prevails in chronic bronchitis, the diet should be nutritious, and early and regular hours observed; mustard plasters, and occasionally blisters, should be applied to the chest and between the shoulders. Warm stimulating expectorants should be given, namely, solution of acetate of ammonia, two ounces; carbonate of ammonia, half a drachm; sweet spirits of nitre, three drachms; water, four ounces; two tablespoonfuls to the dose, as occasion requires. to assist the expectoration, and relieve the difficulty of breathing, the steam of warm water may be inhaled. The vapor of spirits of turpentine may be diffused about the apartment by putting a tablespoonful in a teacupful of hot water poured in a flat dish. The use of a respirator during the winter months is a valuable means of warding off the attacks of the disease.

Burns. These are of a serious character, a surgeon should at once be sent for; meanwhile, it is important to preserve as much as possible the underneath skin.

Treatment: The best application is flour dusted on the injured part with a common kitchen-dredger; and as the blisters rise, let the water be carefully drawn off, and the flour again applied. Or: Apply cotton-wool to the part immediately after the accident, and allow it to remain until the pain has entirely ceased, or until the wool drops off with the scarf-skin.

Chapped Hands. This troublesome complaint arises generally from not wiping the hands perfectly dry after washing them.

Treatment: Borax, two scruples; glycerine, half ounce; water, seven and a half ounces. Mix and apply as a lotion twice a day.

Child Crowing. A complaint which generally accompanies teething, and which manifests itself by a crowing noise, attended often with a sudden difficulty of breathing approaching suffocation.

Treatment: If connected with teething, the gums should be freely lanced. Cold water should be sprinkled or dashed in the face. If the feet and hands be much convulsed, the child should be placed in a hot bath. During the recurrence of the paroxysms one or two drops of chloric ether may be given every four hours. At the same time the following mixture should be given, with or without the rhubarb, according to the state of the bowels: carbonate of magnesia, ten grains; carbonate of soda, fifteen grains; powdered rhubarb, ten grains; sugar, one drachm; dill-water, two ounces; a teaspoonful once or twice a day. Beyond this, pure air, exercise, and careful feeding alone are necessary.

Chilblains. A species of inflammation that arises from exposure to a severe degree of cold. For Unbroken Chilblains use: solution of acetate of lead and camphorated spirits, of each equal parts; mix, and apply twice a day with hair pencil.

Broken Chilblains. Apply a bread-and-water or linseed-meal poultice, for three or four days in succession, and afterwards dress the sore surface with resin ointment thinly spread on lint, or with an ointment made of equal parts of the ointment of nitrate of mercury and white cerate, applied in the same manner.

Cholera. The first and most common form of this disease depends on an excessive secretion of vitiated bile, which gives rise to violent bilious vomiting and purging, often attended with considerable griping pain and cramp in the limbs.

Treatment: Tincture of opium, tincture of camphor, and spirits of turpentine, of each three drachms; oil of peppermint, thirty drops; mix. Dose, one tea-spoonful in brandy and water, for the mild form of cholera; and one table-spoonful for the more virulent. This proved one of the most effective and popular remedies during the terrible visitation of this disease in the year 1849.

Another Treatment: Chalk mixture; one ounce aromatic confection, ten to fifteen grains; tincture of opium, five to fifteen drops. To be taken every three or four hours until the looseness ceases.

A Preventive: Bicarbonate of soda, one scruple; ginger, eight grains; in a glass of water after breakfast and supper.

Cold in the Head. A complaint arising from inflammation of the lining membrane of the nostrils.

Treatment for a Slight Cold: On going to bed take a basin of warm gruel, arrowroot, barley water or any other warm drink, and bathe the feet in hot water for at least twenty minutes.

Treatment for a Severe Cold: The patient should remain in a room as nearly as possible of uniform temperature, bathe the feet in water as hot as it can be borne, with some mustard added to it, and take one of the following soporific draughts at bedtime: Sweet spirits of nitre, one drachm; paregoric elixir, one drachm; spirits of mendererus, two drachms; camphor mixture, one ounce; mix. Or Dover's Powder, fifteen grains; spirit of mendererus, half an ounce; cinnamon water, two ounces; mix.

Cold in the Chest. For this complaint the same remedies are to be applied as for cold in the head, with the addition of mustard plasters to the chest.

Cold Feet. The derangement is attributable to defective circulation of the blood. Coldness of the feet mostly comes on at night, and will often prevent a person sleeping long after he has got into bed.

Treatment: Half an hour before bed-time walk up and down the room briskly, or run up and down stairs. Rub the feet with the hand or a flesh-brush. Dip them into hot water, with suffering them to remain in any length of time. Drink some warm beverage just before going to bed. In winter-time, wear boots instead of slippers in the house. Do not sit long together, but every now and then get up and walk about. These and many other simple expedients, may be adopted to prevent this unpleasant sensation.

Colic. This disease depends on spasmodic and irregular contraction of the muscular structure of the bowels. It is indicated by griping pains in the bowels, chiefly about the navel, and often accompanied with a painful distension of the whole of the lower region of the bowels, with vomiting and costiveness.

Treatment: Apply warmth to the feet in all cases. Put a strong mustard plaster over the whole of the stomach, and foment with poppy-heads and chamomiles.

Or: Give a tea-spoonful of antimonial wine every quarter hour in warm water, till the stomach is thoroughly relieved of its contents; four hours afterwards administer an ounce of castor-oil.

Painter's Colic is characterized by obstinate costiveness, and vomiting of acrid bile; the pains come on in paroxysms. The spasms gradually become more violent, and if not frequently alleviated, the bowels become perfectly intractable.

Treatment: Give immediately from thirty to forty drops of laudanum, and apply a hot bath; afterwards give the following mixture: take of sulphate of magnesia one ounce; powdered alum two drachms; tincture of opium, half a drachm; water, six ounces; one-fourth every four hours.

Consumption. A disease resulting from a scrofulous state of the constitution, which especially determines to the lungs. It would be folly to attempt to give remedies for a complaint so difficult of treatment; and we will therefore content ourselves with a few brief and general observations. Medicines of all kinds have in turn been vaunted as specific remedies for consumption: acids, alkalies, turpentines, vegetable and mineral tonics, various sedatives and narcotics, cod-liver oil, &c. Under suitable circumstances any of these medicines may be available, but attention to air, exercise, diet, and general regimen, will often do more towards improving the system than all the medicines that can be administered. We may venture to assert that consumption is curable in its early stages, and in its more advanced states it may be alleviated or arrested. Much may be done at the onset of the disease by careful examination as to its cause and origin; and as it is decidedly a disease of debility, the grand aim should be to discover the means by which the constitution may be strengthened and improved.

Constipation. Another form of costiveness, generally resolving itself into an habitual state of the system.

Treatment: Regulate the bowels carefully, if possible, without the aid of medicine, by soliciting their action daily, and taking mixed diet. Where the bowels are weak, uneasy, torpid, and where there is a general sense of coldness, and some aperient is absolutely required, have recourse to the following: Tincture of rhubarb and tincture of senna, of each two drachms; potash water or sal-volatile, half a drachm; mix in a wine-glassful of camomile tea, and take it every day at noon or an hour before dinner, gradually reducing the dose, or leaving it off by degrees. See **Costiveness.**

Convulsions are of various kinds, partial or general, most commonly displayed in children by the muscle of the glove of the eye, throwing the ball into involuntary distortions, the face, neck and jaws are similarly affected; the legs drawn stiffly up, and on a sudden, violently thrust down again; the arms act without control, or remain stiff and motionless. It is a complaint incidental to teething.

Treatment: Put the child into a warm bath ten to fifteen minutes; and administer to a child from six months to a year and a-half old, five drops of antimonial wine in a teaspoonful of water, repeating the dose every two and a-half hours till the child falls asleep; when it awakens, give one grain of calomel and one of loaf sugar, and at the expiration of four hours, a teaspoonful of castor oil. If the age from two to five years, increase the dose proportionately.

Corns. A thickened state of the scarf-skin, caused by pressure or friction. The part of the skin acted upon becomes hard, and presses upon the sensible skin within, which, endeavoring to relieve itself, produces an additional quantity of scarf-skin.

Treatment: Soak the feet in warm water, pare the top of the corn, and apply one of the following solvents: 1. Lunar caustic. Moisten the corn, and rub it with the caustic. 2. Nitric acid, applied with a rod or stick. 3. Strong solution of sub-carbonate of potash. The corn is gradually eaten away and disappears.

As corns are the result of friction, they may be prevented or driven away at an early stage by anointing them every night and morning with sweet oil, on the same principle that lubrication is applied to axle-trees, &c., to prevent friction injuring them.

Costiveness. An undue retention of the contents of the stomach, in which they are unusually hard, and expelled with difficulty and sometimes with pain.

Treatment: Adopt a diet free from all astringents, taking care especially that there is no alum in the bread, and using a coarser kind; let the food consist of a due admixture of meat and vegetables for dinner; the beverage water, light malt liquor, or occasionally spruce beer; for those who drink wine, white wine in preference to port. For breakfast, stale bread or dry toast, with a moderate quantity of butter, honey, fish, or bacon; cocoa, perhaps, is preferable to tea or coffee; and porridge made with Scotch oatmeal, probably better still. Regular exercise, either by walking or on horseback, should be taken. Roasted or boiled apples, pears, stewed prunes, raisins, gruel with currants, broths with spinach, leeks, and other soft pot-herbs, are excellent laxatives. If the above mode of living fail to relax the bowels, inject warm water by means of an enema. If there be an objection to the use of the foregoing, take of castor-oil four parts, and of tincture of jalap, aloes or rhubarb, one part; mix and diligently rub over the region of the stomach every morning before rising; it should be done under the bedclothes, lest the unpleasant odor should sicken the stomach.

Coughs. The common complaint results from the irritation of the air-passages, which may originate in various causes. The most common cough is that arising from a cold.

Treatment: Observe light diet, take a dose of salts and senna in the morning; at night put the feet and legs into warm water, and immediately after drying get into bed, drink a pint of hot whey, with three grains of nitre in it. Cover up warmer than usual, in order to encourage perspiration; and dry the skin thoroughly before rising. Or take: Syrup of poppies, syrup of squills, and paregoric equal parts; mix. Dose, a table-spoonful when the cough is troublesome.

Cramp. An affection usually caused by exposure to cold and damp.

Treatment: Foment the part affected with warm water, with a little mustard mixed in it; drink nothing cold, and take a little brandy and water; put the feet in warm water, and endeavor to produce a perspiration, take two or three times a day a dose of Peruvian bark in a little wine, or a little ginger and water. For severe cases: Take of strong liniment of ammonia, one and a-half ounces; oil of turpentine, one ounce; spirits of camphor, one ounce; hard soap, four drachms, mix the whole well together, and apply it to the part on flannels heated and moistened. For cramps in the stomach: Drink copious draughts of hot water, brandy and water, ether or laudanum; apply hot flannels moistened with compound camphor liniment and turpentine; bathe the feet in warm water, or apply mustard poultices to them. When the cause of cramp is constitutional, the best preventives are warm tonics, such as the essence of ginger and camomile, Jamaica ginger in powder, etc., avoiding fermented liquor and green vegetable, particularly for supper, and wearing flannel next the skin.

Croup. An inflammation of the air-passages, peculiar to children. It commences by producing a difficulty of breathing, and the breath passes with a harsh rasping noise which can be heard from one room to another. Those who have had one attack are subject to others, and it is very apt to run in families. It is very rapid in its course, and has been known to terminate fatally within an hour or two from the first attack; a most important point, therefore, is to adopt remedial measures with promptitude and energy.

Treatment: Immediately the sound previously described is recognized, give from half to a whole teaspoonful of antimonial wine every quarter of an hour, until the stomach be freely relieved by vomiting. Afterwards give four grains of calomel in honey, putting it on the tongue by little and little with the tip of the finger, especially if the swallowing be rendered difficult. Put four leeches on each side of the prominent part of the throat, and rub the breast with a few drops of croton oil. If the disease gain ground, put the child into a bath as warm as it can bear, to which a half pound of mustard has been added; keep the child in the bath for twenty minutes, unless it be on the point of fainting. When removed from the bath, apply to the thighs, legs, or feet, mustard poultices, made of equal parts of mustard and hot linseed meal; suffer them to remain on for a quarter of an hour, and let the application be repeated at half-hour intervals six or eight times. Should this treatment afford relief, and the breathing become a little easier, the calomel and antimonial wine will begin to clear the intestines, and an amendment may be looked for. The best now to be done is to rub the throat with croton oil (avoiding the leech bites), which will bring out a plentiful crop of small pimples; and give ten drops of antimonial wine with eight drops of the tincture of henbane every three hours. If a visible improvement should take place by the fourth night, give two grains of calomel and four grains of powdered scammony, succeeded on the following morning by a black draught, formed of twenty grains of manna, two drachms of Epsom salts, and one ounce of infusion of senna. When the child has recovered, give it every other morning for a month, four grains calcined magnesia, twenty drops tincture of ginger and camomile, and one drachm Epsom salts, in one ounce infusion of cascarilla. Ever after let the child wear flannel next the skin.

Deafness. The most frequent cause of this disorder is cold, causing a lodgment of hardened wax in the outer passage of the ear.

Treatment: Drop into the ear every night a small portion of salad oil, and syringe the ear daily with warm water till the wax is detached and washed out; then apply a little wool or cotton, moistened with the following liniment: camphorated oil, half an ounce; soap-liniment, half-drachm; mix. Continue this for some weeks.

Debility is a falling off from the usual power of the individual to perform those exertions in which he has been habitually engaged.

Treatment: Nourishing food, change of air, careful regulation of diet, cold shower baths, and the following forms of medicine: Sulphate of magnesia, four ounces; sulphate of iron, eight grains; sulphate of quinine, ten grains; diluted sulphuric acid, one drachm; infusion of gentian root, eight ounces; two tablespoonfuls twice or thrice a day.

Or, compound tincture of bark, one ounce; carbonate of ammonia, two scruples; water, eight ounces, two tablespoonfuls three times a day.

Depression of Spirits. This distressing state may depend on excessive exhaustion of nervous power, from anxiety, disappointment, or undue mental exertion. It may also originate in bilious affection or derangement of the general health, and these little causes often enter into combination with those first mentioned.

Treatment: The first thing is to turn the attention and thoughts from those objects and channels which have proved prejudicial; then endeavor to brace up the nerves, and gain tone for the general system by exercise on horseback or on foot, by regulated diet, and by early hours. Indolence and luxurious living should be avoided, active employment resorted to, and the mind engaged in some pursuit which will afford interest as well as employment. With regard to medical treatment, the state of the bowels must be attended to, which in these cases are often torpid and inactive. To remedy this, the following should be taken: Extract of aloes, thirty grains; Castile soap, twenty grains; oil of cloves, three drops; mix, divide into twelve pills, and take one or two for a dose, according to circumstances.

Or, powdered aloes and powdered gum-guaiacum, of each forty grains; extract of henbane, half-drachm; mix, and divide into thirty pills, two to be taken when required. The diet should be nutritious and somewhat generous; meat may be eaten twice a day, and a moderate amount of stimulating fluids taken. Tea and coffee in excess should be avoided.

Diarrhoea. A disease which consists of frequent and copious discharge of feculent matter from the intestines, accompanied with griping and vomiting, but without inflammation.

Treatment: When diarrhoea proceeds from over-eating, from irritating or unwholesome food, or from constipation of the bowels, it is then, an effort of nature to expel the offending matter, and ought not, therefore, to be checked abruptly by astringent remedies, which, though of great service when judiciously used, are often given indiscriminately in all cases of this disorder, which they frequently aggravate, or bring on others of a more serious character. When the disorder arises simply from an effort of nature, as described, take the following: Rhubarb in powder, 15 grains; Henry's magnesia, one scruple; cinnamon water, one and a -half ounce; compound tincture of lavender, half-drachm; mix and take at once. When the complaint is obstinate and severe, chalk mixture, six ounces; aromatic confection, one drachm; tincture of cinnamon, two drachms; laudanum, forty drops; mix; two tablespoonfuls to be taken after every liquid evacuation. If the foregoing should fail, take tincture of catechu, three-quarters of an ounce; aromatic confection, one drachm; chalk mixture, six ounces; laudanum, forty drops; syrup of ginger, half an ounce; mix; one or two tablespoonfuls to be taken after every loose evacuation.

For Children. In children from one year to five years old, if diarrhoea be not habitual, but merely accidental, the best treatment is, from half to a teaspoonful of antimonial wine every quarter of an hour till the stomach has been thoroughly relieved; and at bedtime, from two to four grains of powdered mercury with chalk, succeeded on the following morning by a draught made of five grains of calcined magnesia and twenty grains of manna, in one ounce of peppermint water.

Dropsy. An unnatural formation of fluid beneath the skin, or in some cavities of the body. the treatment will vary according to the situation and action of the effusion, and with the organ which is implicated. The causes are often too obscure, and the proper and efficient remedies too active to be entrusted to non-medical hands, particularly as it can rarely be an emergency. Whatever form dropsy assumes, the case should at once be put under medicals superintendence. As temporary palliative measures, the bowels should be kept either simply open or actively purged, according as the patient is of weak or strong habit of body; and the effusion of water by drinking of such medicines and liquors as increase the action of the kidneys, as broom, dandelion, parsley, or gin. [Juniper berries or the liquor? Ed]

Dysentery. An inflammatory disease of the large intestines. It occurs in the summer and autumn, and is most common in warm countries. The common causes of it are unwholesome diet, excessive fatigue, and exposure to the night air.

Treatment: In mild cases, two or three doses of castor oil, half an ounce to one ounce; Epsom salts, half an ounce, accompanied by, and followed up with pills or powders of ipecacuhana, calomel, and opium, of each one grain, at intervals of two or four hours, will usually be found a satisfactory mode of treatment. Warm baths or hot fomentations to the stomach are useful adjuncts, as are also small injections of a teacupful of thin starch, with twenty or thirty drops of laudanum, thrown up into the bowel at intervals of a few hours; any tendency to constipation must be obviated by the taking of Epsom salts or castor oil. A light farinaceous diet should be observed. A recumbent position while the disease is active is desirable. The after debility is best treated with such bitters as cascarilla, columba, and bark.

Epilepsy. This disease arises from a disorder of the brain and spinal cord, the affection either originating directly in them, or through them in consequence of irritation in some portion of the body. When the fit comes on, the patient drops suddenly, and utters a piercing shriek; this is followed by a fit, which lasts a few minutes, and is succeeded by a torpor of some hours' duration.

Treatment: As epileptic subjects are apt to do themselves injury during the continuance of the fit, this must be specially guarded against, and may best be done by wrapping a large blanket or rug round the patient; while to prevent the tongue being bitten, a piece of india-rubber or wood should be placed between the teeth, or the mouth may be filled with common salt. Lay the patient on a bed with the head slightly raised, loosen the neck-cloth and the clothes about the neck and chest. If the head be hot, pour cold water upon it; and if the feet are cold, immerse them in a foot-bath of hot water and mustard, as soon as the violence of the fit is passed. An emetic should then be given if the stomach is gorged, and the patient should then be suffered to remain tranquil until he recovers.

Eruptions of the Skin. Under this head may be included all rashes not especially treated of in this little work.

Treatment: As the main source of eruptions are derangements of the constitution and stomach, it must be borne in mind that local applications for restoring the healthy action of the skin, such as daily warm and cold sponging, warm baths, vapor baths, and well-regulated exercise, should be adopted, together with the following: Take of blue pill twenty grains; camphor, six grains; tartarised antimony, one grain; mix, and divide into sixteen pills, one or two to be taken every night for three or four nights successively; to be stopped for a like period, and then renewed. If the bowels do not act gently under the influence of these, a teaspoonful of Epsom slats and carbonate of magnesia, mixed in equal proportions, may be taken each following morning.

Exhaustion. The diminished power either of the body generally, or of one or more of its organs, to continue its natural active operations, until it has been recruited by a period of repose. As this derangement is commonly induced by excess of labor or continued exertion, in these cases the stomach is not receiving its full supply of nervous stimulation, and therefore its work must be made as light as possible, consistent with conveying good nourishment into the system; small quantities of food should be taken at a time, and more frequently repeated. In the majority of instances, the most efficient nourishment will be strong concentrated animal soup, either alone or with bread; and next in utility will be coffee or cocoa, along with bread or biscuit, or with the yolk of an egg beaten into them. The use of wines and spirits should be avoided as long as possible. But if extreme exhaustion exist, these latter will be found excellent agents for restoring the vital powers. A warm bath is also very gratefuls and efficacious in cases of exhaustion. Occasional doses of the following will stand in good stead: Peppermint water, one and a-half ounce; salvolatile, half a drachm; sweet spirit of nitre, twelve drops; compound spirit of lavender, one drachm; syrup of cloves, half an ounce; mix. Dose, two tablespoonfuls. Or, camphor julep, one drachm; Hoffman's ether, two drachms; compound tincture of cardamoms, half an ounce; spirit of aniseed, six drachms; oil of caraway, ten drachms; syrup of ginger, two drachms, peppermint water, five and a-half ounces; mix. Dose, two tablespoonfuls.

Eyes, Weakness of. Sulphate of copper, fifteen grains; camphor, four grains; boiling water, four ounces; mix, strain, and when cold, make up to four pints with water; bathe the eye night and morning with a portion of the mixture.

Face-Ache. Dip a sponge, or piece of flannel, into boiling water, and apply it as hot as can be borne over the site of the pain.

Or: Soak a piece of lint in chloroform, and apply it over the affected part. Rub in laudanum.

Fainting. During the fit, the nostrils must be stimulated by smelling salts, and cold water sprinkled over the face and chest, and free air allowed. If the fainting be from loss of blood, the patient should be placed on his back, without any elevation of the head; and when the patient can swallow, a little warm wine should be placed in his mouth.

Or: let the patient smell vinegar, and at the same time bathe his temples, forehead, and wrists with vinegar mixed with an equal quantity of warm water; and if he can swallow, pour into his mouth two or three spoonfuls of vinegar mixed with four or five times as much warm water.

Freckles. These are of two kinds: Summer freckles, resulting from the action of the sun and heat during the summer season, and Cold freckles, which occur at all times of the year, and are chiefly confined to persons of fair complexion.

Treatment: Borax, fifteen grains; lemon juice, one ounce; sugar candy, half a drachm; mix the powders with the juice, and let them stand in a bottle, shaking them occasionally until they are dissolved. Or take Muriate of ammonia, one drachm; spring water, one pint; lavender water, two drachms. Apply with a sponge two or three times a day.

Frost-Bite. Lengthened exposure to the cold is apt to render parts of the body numb and inanimate; the fingers, toes, lips, nose, and ears, are especially liable to be affected.

Treatment: To restore the natural warmth of the body gradually must be the main object, and on no account must a considerable degree of heat be applied suddenly, as it would either kill the part outright, or cause violent inflammation to result. Friction with snow or cold water merely should be used, until the circulation is somewhat restored, and then equal parts of brandy or some other spirit mixed with cold water may be applied, until the restoration is completed. Frost-bites are apt to leave troublesome sores, which are difficult to heal. The red precipitate ointment is the best application; and if much inflamed, they should be poulticed.

Gravel. A disease depending on the formation of stony matter in the kidney.

Treatment: The general treatment should consist in a hot bath and warm fomentations; a dose of castor-oil should be administered, and when the bowels have acted, if there be much pain, the following may be given: Solution of acetate of morphine, one drachm; spirit of hydrochloric ether, two drachms; syrup of roses, half an ounce; camphor mixture, four ounces; mix. Dose: one-fourth part, to be taken at bedtime. Linseed tea or barley water should be drank freely.

Hair, Weakness of. The falling off of hair is generally a sign of debility of constitution.

Treatment: The removal of the weakness, and the general bracing up of the system, is the first step to take. Frequent cutting and frequent brushing and washing, are the next methods. In addition to this, there may be applied, every morning and evening, a portion of the following lotion: Eau-de-cologne, two ounces; tincture of cantharides, two drachms; oil of rosemary, ten drops; oil of lavender, ten drops; mix.

Or: Clean the hair with rum every night on a soft brush, then comb it very gently, and pour cold water on the head every morning, after which thoroughly dry it. A drop or two of sweet-oil twice a week should also be used.

Hairs, Grey. The sedentary, the studious, the debilitated, and the sickly, are, with very few exceptions, those who are earliest visited with grey hair. All whose employment renders much sitting necessary, and little or no exercise possible, are most liable to carry grey hairs.

Treatment: Mix thoroughly a small quantity of sub-nitrate of bismuth with any common pomatum, and brush a small portion of it into the hair daily.

Headache. This painful malady, whether it be bilious, nervous, inflammatory, or plethoric, owes its origin generally to one cause, namely, constipation. The readiest and most certain means of cure, therefore, is to restore regularity in the functions of the bowels.

Treatment: Let the food be light, and at dinner especially moderate; drink only a little weak brandy and water, take gentle exercise; retire to rest at a certain hour every night. Take of the mass of blue pill one drachm, and divide it into twelve pills, one or two for a dose every second night. In the morning, before breakfast, take of Epsom salts a quarter of an ounce; sub-carbonate of potash, one scruple; dissolve them in a wine-glassful of cold water, with a little loaf sugar. Put the mixture into a large glass and add a tablespoonful of lemon-juice. Drink it while it is frothing up. Persist in the treatment for a fortnight, when the pills may be given at more distant intervals; and at the end of another fortnight they may be discontinued altogether. The morning draught may be continued for a few mornings, by which time the bowels will have, in all probability, recovered their natural action.--If the headache be not removed by the foregoing treatment, the following should be adopted: Commence by taking of jalap thirty grains, and calomel five grains, divided into two powders one of the powders to be taken two hours before the other. When this purgative has operated well, bathe the legs in warm water; then take three grains of antimonial powder, and lie down in bed with the head elevated. Put two small blisters either on the side near the temples or behind the ears, according to the situation of the pain. A light diet should at the same time be observed. The diet should be as follows: For breakfast, an egg, one slice of bread and butter, and one cup of tea; for dinner, a mutton chop, or an equal quantity of roast meat, with a thick slice of bread; for tea, a cupful of tea and a little dry toast; for supper, a little bread and butter, with wine and water. Eat neither veal, pork, bacon, pastry, pudding, fruit, nor vegetables. Drink nothing at dinner; but one hour afterwards half a tumbler of barley water. Take four hours' exercise in the open air daily, and regulate the bowels with the following mixture: Epsom salts, two drachms; sulphate of iron, four grains. Battley's liquid dandelion, half an ounce; diluted sulphuric acid, forty-eight drops; water, five and a-half ounces; mix, and take three tablespoonfuls twice a day. The pursuance of this simple plan will in most cases remove and prevent headache.

Heart, Palpitation of. Palpitation of the heart may arise from a variety of causes, such as sudden fear, excitement, flatulence, running, stimulants, &c. When it is habitual, or lasts for any time, it generally depends upon a disordered stomach; in any case the complaint need not give rise to aggravated fears, for when organic disease of the heart exists, it is a singular fact, that the patient is unconscious of any unusual action; whereas any person putting his hand upon the chest can detect distinctly the irregular throbs. The palpitation of the heart is most common with persons of nervous temperament and weakly constitution, for their delicate frames are more susceptible to the action going on within.

Treatment: The aim in this case should be to brace up and invigorate the system, generous diet, exercise employment mental and bodily and a course of tonics. This system, if persevered in, will speedily conquer the derangement.

Treatment: Sometimes palpitation of the heart exists with persons of full habit of body; and in such cases the diet should be lowered, the ordinary amount of exercise increased, and gentle purgatives of a warm and soothing nature resorted to.

Heartburn. What is commonly called heartburn is not a disease of the heart, but an uneasy sensation of heat or acrimony about the pit of the stomach, accompanied, sometimes, by a rising in the throat like water.

Treatment: One teaspoonful of the spirit of nitrous ether, in a glass of water or a cup of tea.

Or: A large teaspoon of magnesia, taken in a wineglass of water. Take this two or three times a day.

Hysterics. This complaint is confined, chiefly to females.

Treatment: A fit of hysterics is generally the result of some natural and immediate cause, and until this is discovered and removed, the patient will always be subject to these fits. When a person is seized with the fit the dress should be loosened, fresh air admitted, cold water dashed in the face, and salts, or singed feathers, applied to the nostrils. If consciousness does not then return, a draught of sal-volatile and water should be given, and if the patient be still insensible, the temples, and the nape of the neck should be rubbed with brandy. When hysterics can be traced to impaired natural action, equal portions of pennyroyal and wormwood should be steeped in boiling water, and suffered to simmer by the fire until the virtue of the herbs is extracted. It should then be allowed to cool, and half a pint be taken twice or thrice a day, succeeded on each occasion by a compound assafoetida pill, until the desired relief is afforded.

Indigestion. This is one of the most common ailments to which mankind are subject, there being few individuals who have not experienced it oftener than once in their lives. Accidental fits of indigestion are of frequent occurrence, and arise for the most part from overloading the stomach with food, and indulging too freely in wine, spirits, or other intoxicating liquors. Confirmed or chronic indigestion may depend on debility or want of tone of the stomach, or it may be caused by the lining or mucous membrane of this organ being in a state of irritation or chronic inflammation. One of the most frequent causes of indigestion is not masticating the food we eat properly, by which such food is bolted instead of being reduced to a natural pulp, thereby presenting to the digestive organs a hardened mass, which it has the greatest difficulty to operate upon. Another cause us habitual inattention to diet, both as regards the quality and quantity of food, irregularity in the times of eating, drinking large quantities of relaxing fluids, and using malt liquors too freely. A third cause is insufficient exercise; a fourth cause, impure air; and besides these, there are numberless other causes which in a greater or lesser degree exercise their baneful influence upon this vital and all-important function of our natures. Before we proceed to give the remedies applicable to this disorder, we will lay before our readers what is of equal consequence, both as regards prevention and cure namely.

Treatment: Rise early; sponge the body freely with cold water; breakfast without taking previous exercise, except a saunter in the garden. At breakfast, drink no more than half a pint of tea, neither too strong nor too weak, and black tea in preference to any other. Eat a slice or two of stale bread, together with a rasher of streaky bacon. After a short rest, exercise should then be taken for two hours or upwards. The dinner hour should be not later than four or five hours after breakfast, and the best time in the day for this meal is one or two o'clock. The food should be plain, without sauces. Roast mutton is the best of all meats, both as regards its nourishing properties and the ease with which it can be digested. For drink, toast and water, and tea, weak, are preferable. After dinner, rest and quiet for an hour are desirable. About three or four hours after dinner, a cup of tea with a biscuit. Supper at nine on light food, with a draught of ale or wine and water. To bed between ten and eleven o'clock This mode of living will generally render a person exempt from habitual indigestion; nevertheless, in spite of these precautions, occasional attacks of this derangement will make themselves felt.

Treatment: Bay berries, six drachms; grains of paradise, two drachms; socotrine aloes, and filings of iron, of each two scruples; oil of turpentine, two drachms; simple syrup, sufficient for an electuary: Take a piece the size of a nutmeg night and morning.

Influenza. There is perhaps scarcely any complaint which attacks a person so suddenly, and at the same time so severely, as influenza. It generally comes on by an intense feeling of pain at the top of the head, accompanied with alternate sensation of heat and cold, cough, violent sneezing, running at the nostrils, eyes, &c.

Treatment: The patient should remain in a warm room, or keep his bed if very poorly; hot bricks or hot-water bottles should be applied to the feet, and mustard poultices to the chest. The bowels should be kept gently open, and weak wine-whey should be given, each pint having mixed with it a grain of tartar emetic and a drachm of nitrate of potash; a wine-glassful of this every four hours. Meanwhile the diet should be light and yet nutritious; a little mutton broth for dinner, with sago or arrowroot, and a small quantity of wine at other times. As the feverishness which attends this complaint abates, a tonic should be administered as follows: Infusion of gentian, one ounce; carbonate of ammonia, five grains. Take three times a day.

Jaundice. A disease arising from obstruction to the passage of the bile into the intestines, from disorders of the liver.

Treatment: The diet should be cool, light, and diluting, consisting chiefly of ripe fruit and mild vegetables. The drink., barley-water or linseed tea, sweetened with liquorice; the bowels must be kept gently open. When the disease has abated, constant doses of Peruvian bark should be given, with good port wine, plenty of exercise taken, and a mustard poultice occasionally placed over the liver.

Lumbago. A rheumatic affection of the muscles of the loins. It is indicated by stiffness and pain, and the pain is aggravated by stooping, sitting, or rising to the upright posture. It is most generally caused by exposure to wet or cold.

Treatment: Nothing affords greater relief than hot moist applications to the back, continued from twelve to twenty-four hours at a time, and followed by the rubbing well into the back and loins of soap liniment, combined with one-sixth part of turpentine. Take also at bedtime ten grains of Dover's powder, with two grains of calomel, and on the following morning half an ounce of castor-oil. Take also twice a day ten grains of carbonate of potass, with one teaspoonful of sweet nitre, in a wine-glassful of water.

Mouth (Sore). Take of honey two tablespoonfuls; borax, powdered, half-drachm; mix well together and take a teaspoonful twice a day. The mixture should be placed in the mouth little by little, touching the various ulcers that are visible, or can be got at.

Mumps. These are swellings of the glands under the jaw, the ear, and down the neck. They render the act of swallowing difficult, and are attended with a slight degree of feverishness, foul tongue, and headache.

Treatment: Apply warm fomentations to the swelling, and immediately afterwards wrap round with flannel to prevent cold-chilling; sprinkle compound liniment of turpentine. Let the diet be light, chiefly farinaceous, and keep the bowels regular by employing mild aperients. After the fourth day, take one grain of quinine, in fifteen drops of diluted vitriolic acid, in a wine-glass of water, three times a day for a fortnight. Should the swellings suddenly disappear, and thereby aggravate the symptoms of fever, the following liniment must be applied: Camphorated spirits, one ounce; solution of sub-carbonate of ammonia, two drachms; tincture of cantharides, half-drachm; mix, and rub in until the swellings re-appear. Take also internally, nitrate of potass, one drachm; tartarised antimony, one and a half grain. Mix and divide into six powders, one of which is to be taken every four hours. Caution. This disease is contagious either by the atmosphere or personal contact.

Nausea. A sensation of sickness, with an inclination to vomit. Although the feeling of nausea itself is referred to the stomach, and may be due to causes connected with that organ, it also frequently originates in disorder in other and distant parts of the body.

Treatment: Clear the stomach by an emetic of ipecacuhana, and afterwards the bowels by two or three grains of calomel at night, followed by a black draught in the morning; also take hydrocyanic acid, in doses of one to three drops, with five grains of bicarbonate of soda, every two, three or four hours, in a glass of water. If the foregoing should fail, two or three leeches may be applied to the pit of the stomach, and one grain of calomel, with three grains of chalk or magnesia, laid on the tongue in powder, and swallowed gradually every four or six hours. So long as the stomach is in a state of irritation, only small quantities of food should be introduced into it at one time, as a teaspoonful of milk or beef tea every hour.

Nail, Ingrowing. It often happens that a tight or ill-made shoe, by continued pressure on one part of the nail, forces it into the flesh, and then causes great pain and inconvenience.

Treatment for the Toe: First procure an easier shoe, which will allow the nail to take its natural course; then take a piece of glass, and with it scrape the whole length of the middle of the nail persistently, and yet with a delicate hand. By this means, the centre of the nail will eventually be rendered so thin, that it may be readily bent, and in this flexible condition it gives way to the upward pressure of the skin on its outward edges, readily bends, and offers no further resistance. The cause of irritation being withdrawn, the tenderness soon heals, and the proud flesh drops down.

Observe: An ingrowing nail may be caused by an improper mode of cutting it. Nails should never be clipped at the corners, but cut straight across the top, if anything, slightly scooped in the middle. This leaves a sufficient amount of resistance at the corners; for wear what shoes we may, there must always be a certain degree of pressure on the nail, which should by provided for.

Treatment for the Finger: Wrap the affected finger in a compress moistened with a lotion made as follows: Liquor of ammonia, one ounce; camphorated alcohol, one drachm; bay salt, quarter of an ounce; water, three quarters of a pint; mix and shake well together. After ten minutes, remove this, and replace it by a compress anointed with camphor pomatum, and kept in place till next dressing by an india-rubber finger-stall drawn over it. Then dissolve one and a quarter ounces of camphor in a gill of brandy, wet a narrow band with this solution, place it round the root of the nail, and let it remain there until the next dressing.

Observe: The finger nails should be cut of an oval shape, corresponding with the form of the finger; they should not be allowed to grow too long, as they thereby are rendered more liable to accident, neither should they be too short, as they thus deprive the ends of the fingers of their protection and support. When the nails are naturally ragged or ill-formed, they should be gently scraped, afterwards rubbed with lemon, then rinsed with water, and well dried with a towel. If the nails grow more to one side than the other, they should be cut in such a manner as to make the points come as near as possible to the centre at the end of the finger.

Nervousness. This unhealthy state of system depends upon general debility. It is often inherited from birth, and as often brought on by excess of sedentary occupation, overstrained employment of the brain, mental emotion, dissipation and excess. The nerves consist of a structure of fibres or cords passing through the entire body, branching off from, and having a connexion with each other, and finally with centres of the brain. They are the organs of feeling and sensation of every kind; and through them the mind operates upon the body. It is obvious, therefore, that what is termed "the nervous system" has an important part in the bodily functions; and upon them, not only much health, but of happiness, depends.

Treatment: The cure of nervous complaints lies rather in moral than in medical treatment. For although much good may be effected by tonics, such as bark, quinine, &c., there is far more benefit to be derived from attention to diet and regimen. In such cases, solid food should preponderate over liquid, and the indulgence in warm and relaxing fluids should be especially avoided; plain and nourishing meat, as beef or mutton, a steak or chop, together with half a pint of bitter ale or stout forming the best dinner. Cocoa is preferable to tea; vegetables should be but sparingly eaten. Sedentary pursuits should be cast aside as much as possible, but where they are compulsory, every spare moment should be devoted to out-door employment and brisk exercise. Early bedtime and early rising will prove beneficial. and the use of the cold shower bath is excellent. Gymnastic exercises, fencing, horse-riding, rowing, dancing and other pursuits which call forth the energies, serve also to brace and invigorate the nervous system. It will also be well to mingle with society, frequent public assemblies and amusement, and thus dispel that morbid desire for seclusion and quietude which, if indulged in to excess, renders a person unfitted for intercourse with mankind, and materially interferes with advancement in life. Above all, nervous patients should avoid seeking the advice of those empirics whose advertisement crowd the columns of our newspapers, whose nostrums are worthless, and who only lay traps for patients in order to pander to their fears and prey upon their weakness. If the patient does not derive the expected benefit by following out the course indicated above, he should place himself under a respectable medical man, who has a reputation to sustain, and a character to lose.

Neuralgia. A painful affection of the nerves, situated chiefly in the face and head; it is also called Tic Douloureux. This disease usually makes itself felt in a series of sharp darting pains, coming on suddenly and as suddenly going away. It may result from a variety of causes, chiefly among which is exposure to damp and cold.

Treatment: Take, in the first instance, a mild aperient, to be followed for the next twenty-four hours with a two-grain pill of quinine every four hours; on the second day, fifteen grains of carbonate of iron in a wine-glassful of water; also every four hours, should the pain continue, apply a bran poultice, sprinkled with turpentine, to the affected part, and at bedtime, in order to procure sleep and dull the pain, twenty-four drops of laudanum may be taken. If the attack is not mitigated in its severity, the following treatment must be adopted: Take of Dover's powder twenty grains; carbonate of ammonia, twelve grains; camphor water, three ounces; spirit of ether, half-a-drachm; mix, and take two tablespoonfuls three times a day; also take of quinine, six grains; carbonate of soda, twelve grains; carbonate of iron, one drachm; mix and divide into three powders, one to be taken an hour after each dose of the foregoing mixture.

Caution: Persons liable to this distressing malady should be careful not to expose themselves to draughts, or wet, or damp. They should also make choice of a high situation, and gravelly soil to reside in.

Nightmare. The common causes of nightmare are indigestion and the use of narcotic and intoxicating substances.

Treatment: Take of carbonate of soda ten grains; compound tincture of cardamoms, three drachms; simple syrup, one drachm; peppermint water, one ounce; mix for a draught to be taken at bedtime.

Caution. Persons subject to this visitation ought carefully to shun all kinds of food likely to prove flatulent or of difficult digestion. Hot and heavy suppers are particularly injurious, as are acids. Excess of sedentary employment should also be avoided.

Paralysis, or Palsy. This disease consists of the loss or diminution of sense or motion, or of both, in one or more parts of the body. The symptoms which precede an attack of paralysis are numberless, like prickling sensation throughout the same limbs.

Treatment: The diet where debility exists must be warm and invigorating, seasoned with spices and condiments, as mustard, horseradish, &c. The drink may be generous wine, or good homebrew ale. Friction with a flesh-brush, or the warm hand, is extremely proper, especially on the parts affected. Blisters may likewise be applied with advantage. When this cannot be done, rub in the liniment of ammonia. One of the best external applications is electricity. The shocks should be directed to the parts affected, and repeated daily for several weeks. Cephalic snuff or anything that makes the patient sneeze, is useful. If the tongue be affected, the patient may gargle his mouth frequently with brandy and mustard; or he may retain a lump of sugar in his mouth, moistened with compound spirits of lavender. The wild valerian root is an excellent medicine in this disease. It may either be taken in an infusion with sage leaves, or half a drachm of it in powder in a glass of wine, three or four times a day. If the patient cannot use the valerian, he may take the following: Compound spirits of ammonia, 1/2 ounce; compound spirits of lavender, 1/2 ounce; tincture of castor, 1/2 ounce; mix, and take forty or fifty drops in a glass of wine three or four times a day. A tablespoonful of mustard seed, taken frequently, is a very good medicine. The patient ought also to chew ginger, cinnamon bark, or other warm spices. He may take every four or six hours, three or four tablespoonfuls of the following mixture: Prepared ammonia, two scruples; compound tincture of cardamoms, one ounce; syrup of orange-peel, one ounce; pennyroyal water, eleven ounces; mix. When an attack is accompanied with faintness, and partial loss of consciousness, a teaspoonful of salvolatile in a little water is as suitable a remedy as any other, and may be repeated once or twice in the course of the first hour or two. In all cases of paralysis, however, the great essential is the most perfect quiet; this and time will prove the best restoratives. As the healthy state returns, exertion of any kind must be very gradually and slowly resumed. As this disease imperatively calls for the assistance of a doctor, we have merely alluded to it in general terms, without attempting to point out specific remedies.

Piles. These consist of small tumors, situated on the extremity of the great gut, called the rectum. The piles are usually accompanied by a sense of weight in the back, loins, and bottom of the belly, together with pain in the head, sickness at the stomach, and flatulence in the bowels. If the tumor break, a quantity of blood is voided, and considerable relief from pain is obtained; but if they continue unbroken, the patient experiences great pain. *Treatment:* Take of lenitive electuary one ounce; four of sulphur, one ounce; jalap, in powder, half-drachm; balsam of copaiba, half-ounce; ginger in powder, half-drachm; cream of tartar, half-ounce; syrup of ginger, a sufficient quantity to make into an electuary; mix. Take a teaspoonful every three hours, until the bowels are freely open; at the same time, make use of the following lotion: Goulard water, six ounces; laudanum, one ounce; mix, and apply to the parts repeatedly. When the piles are very painful and swollen, but discharge nothing, the patient should sit over the steam of hot water. He may also apply a linen cloth, dipped in warm spirits of wine, to the upper part, or make use of bread and milk poultices.

Pimples. These depend upon some derangement of the digestive and other internal organs. *Treatment:* Take of tincture of cardamoms, one drachm; ipecacuhana wine, fifteen drops; flour of sulphur, as much as will lie on a 1/4 dollar; mix the whole with a glass of ginger or elder wine, and take at bedtime; repeat it every second or third night, and at the same time, pay attention to the bowels.

Poison, To Counteract the Effect of. There are four kinds of poisons: Mineral, animal, vegetable, and aerial. The mineral poisons corrode the flesh and produce inflammation. The vegetable generally stupefy, and leave no marked inflammation. The animal generally affect the whole body, and the aerial, the respiratory organs.

MINERAL POISONS, Treatment: First empty the stomach by giving the following emetic: Sulphate of zinc, twenty grains; powdered ipecacuhana, ten grains; mixed in milk. When this has operated, give plenty of barley water, milk, a solution of gum arabic, broth, or olive oil; mix wood ashes with boiling water, allow them to settle and give the lees; or powdered charcoal may be given. For arsenic, lime-water, chalk, and magnesia are recommended. For nitrate of silver, common salt a tablespoonful in a quart of water; half a pint for a dose.

ANIMAL POISONS, Treatment: The parts bitten by a venomous animal should, if possible, be immediately cut out, then immersed in warm water; after which, some caustic application such as nitrate of silver should be made to the entire surface of the wounded part. Brandy, ammonia, and other stimulants, with opiates, should be given. In bites from snakes, the use of ligatures above the bitten part should on no account be neglected.

VEGETABLE POISONS, Treatment: The chief of these poisons are Opium, hemlock, digitalis, belladonna, laurel, and various kinds of fungi. In every case give an emetic immediately. Sometimes the stomach is so torpid that vomiting cannot be produced. In such cases, dashing cold water over the head will frequently rouse the patient and bring on vomiting. In all cases where laudanum or opium has been taken, the patient must be kept constantly roused, and made to walk about between two men, or driven with speed over very rough roads in a cart, on no account must he be allowed to fall asleep. Oxalic acid is often taken by mistake for salts; it acts with fearful rapidity, and the remedies must be immediate to be effectual. The chief antidotes are magnesia, chalk, or mortar or plaster taken from a wall, mixed thick in cold water, and swallowed copiously. After giving any of these antidotes, twenty-four grains of sulphate of zinc may be taken.

AERIAL POISONS, Treatment: The fumes of metals generally produce these. The fumes of charcoal and coke are also poisonous. Immediately on discovering a person who has been suffocated by these fumes, take him into the open air and undress him, so that the air may get to every part of his body; place him in a leaning posture on a chair; after a little time, cover him with flannel, sprinkle the face with vinegar and water, the stomach with cold water, and place the legs in a cold bath. After some time, well rub the body, apply sal-volatile to the nostrils; put him in a warm bed, and keep him quiet. When he is able to swallow, give him a little vinegar and water.

Rheumatism. The characteristics of rheumatism are fever, pain about the parts following the track of the muscles, attacking the knees and large joints in preference to those of the feet and hands, increased by external heat. The disease is distinguished into the chronic (long-standing) and acute (recent), the former having pain only present, without fever or inflammation; the latter having fever and inflammation in a high degree.

Chronic Rheumatism, Treatment: Every symptom of this form of rheumatism proves to be a disease of debility, consequently the mode of treatment must be founded upon this idea. Hence, stimulants of almost all kinds, prove serviceable, together with tonics, warm bathing, &c. Let the patient be clothed in flannel next the skin, and take an aperient pill every night and morning, also take thirty drops of the wine of the seeds of colchicum in camphor julep three times day.

Ringworm. This disease is distinct from Scald-Head, which, however, it somewhat resembles. It may attack any portion of the surface of the body, singly or in numerous spots. It consists of a number of small watery pimples, arranged in the form of a circle, the surrounding surface being partially inflamed.

Treatment: Take a little cooling medicine, and apply a lotion composed of carbonate of potash, two drachms; rose-water, eight ounces. Mix.

Scald-Head. This consists in a peculiar pimply eruption, followed by the formation of matter; the skin breaks, and the matter communicates itself to the adjacent parts, until the whole head becomes affected. The disease usually attacks children, especially those of a scrofulous or weak constitution. It is highly contagious.

Treatment: Carefully remove the hair, and apply to the affected parts night and morning the milder kind of the nitrate of mercury ointment; give an occasional dose of calcined magnesia, from four to eight grains, about three times a week. Pay strict attention to the child's diet which should be mild, and chiefly farinaceous, and on no account should salted meats or stimulating food be eaten.

Scald. In this accident the principle to act upon is, to keep up the heat of the part at first, and bring it down gradually to the ordinary temperature. The first, and most important object, is to protect the surface from the action of the air. For this purpose flour, cotton-wool, or wadding. are the readiest means.

Treatment: Flowers of zinc, calomine powder, and lycopodium, of each one ounce; powdered myrrh, and sugar of lead, of each half a drachm; lard, one and a half ounce; mix, and apply from time to time. Or take lime-water, one part; linseed oil, two parts; shake well together, and apply by lint or linen soaked in it.

Observe: In all cases of scalds, if fever should ensue, gentle laxative medicines ought to be taken. The best are castor oil and Epsom salts.

Scarlet Fever. It is our intention to notice only the milder form of this disease, for when it is severe and malignant it demands the most skillful and judicious treatment on the part of a properly qualified medical man. Mild scarlet fever is distinguished by a rash, which appears in innumerable spots about the face and neck, and on the following day they are seen all over the surface of the body. On the third day, the face, neck and breast, appear redder than usual. About the fourth day, the eruption is at its height; and on the fifth it begins to decline.

Treatment: Keep the patient in a cool, well ventilated room, sponge the surface of the body three or four times a day with tepid vinegar and water, give at first a rhubarb draught, with one drachm of neutral tartrate of potash, keep the bowels open with castor oil, given in the morning, and one-tenth of a grain of extract of belladonna, every four or six hours, in a little water. If the head be hot, apply to it rags dipped in cold vinegar and water. The diet should consist of bread and milk; weak beef tea, or mutton broth, with bread, when it can be swallowed. To allay the thirst, a teaspoonful of raspberry vinegar in a small teacupful of water.

Scrofula. This is the name rather of a constitutional tendency than of a specific complaint. It is the result of a delicate constitution, and is most commonly inherited from sickly or diseased parents. The following are some of the signs of scrofula: In the form of the body there is usually observable a want of muscular development; there is also a general paleness and coldness of the surface of the body, which is owing to feeble circulation. In children, the glands, those of the neck, chest, and belly are the most usual seat of scrofulous disease. In adults, the lungs most generally suffer.

Treatment: The body should be regularly submitted to cold or tepid bathing, in order to promote the healthy functions of the skin. The diet must be carefully regulated, consisting chiefly of animal food, taken at certain intervals; an occasional glass of good beer or wine may be allowed. For children, a very nourishing food may be prepared by boiling a small bag filled with suet in cow's milk. It bears a strong resemblance to goat's milk, but has the advantage of being more astringent. A pure, dry, and temperate atmosphere is the best to live in, and during the summer months and the early autumn, much advantage may be derived from sea-air, combined with sea-bathing. All persons of scrofulous tendency should wear flannel continuously next their skin, it being the best protector of the body from the bad influence of our variable climate. A great variety of drugs have been employed in the treatment of scrofula, but they are all of secondary importance in comparison with the means above recommended. Take iodine, one grain; iodide of potash, two

185

grains; distilled water, eight ounces; mix. To a child under seven years of age a dessert-spoonful of this mixture is to be given three times a day, in half a teacupful of water, sweetened with a little sugar. The dose is to be gradually increased to two tablespoonfuls, and the remedy is to be continued, if no unfavorable symptoms occur, for a period of four or five weeks; its use is then to be suspended, and gentle laxatives are to be administered. After an interval of a fortnight the mixture is to be again administered, commencing with a dessert-spoonful, and gradually augmenting the dose as before. At the expiration of a month, the remedy is again to be discontinued, and again renewed. In this manner, the means of cure may be employed with perfect safety, and continued until the desired end is accomplished.

Scurf. This is a natural formation, produced on every part of the body where hair is found, and chiefly in the hair of the head. It is also known by the name of dandruff.

Treatment: Beat up the yolk of an egg with a pint of clean rainwater. Apply it warm, and afterwards wash the head with warm water.

Scurvy. A disease depending on deterioration of the blood, and generally the result of inappropriate nourishment. It commences with langour and signs of general debility, and great depression of spirits; the gums become swollen and spongy, red or purple looking, project over the teeth, and bleed easily. The lower extremities become at first stiff, then swollen and hard.

Treatment: As the deprivation of fresh vegetable and milk is frequently the cause of this complaint, so, a return to these will overcome the disease; and this of itself is oftentimes a remedy.

Side, Pains in. Pains in the side may arise from rheumatic affections, or from derangement of the stomach.

Treatment: Regulate the state of the bowels with mild aperients, and if the system seems impoverished and there has been much debility of the digestive organs, take twenty grains of the sesquioxide of iron twice or thrice a day. Employ the warm bath frequenly, and apply to the part affected a muslin bag filled with hops and well soaked in hot water; also rub in every fourth hour the following: Tincture of aconite, half an ounce; soap liniment, one and a-half ounces; mix. If the pains be situated high up in the region of the chest, they may be occasioned by inflammatory affection of the lungs, but in this case will be accompanied with more or less fever, and other symptoms indicative of the disorder. Pain on the right side, lower down, may be owing to an affection of the liver; on the left side, an affection to the pain on the right side. It, however, often occurs as a sympathetic affection, sometimes of the heart or lungs, in either sex. It is common in females, at times of functional disorder. Obstinate and increasing pain of the side, which will not go away with the treatment above indicated, must on no account be neglected. There is evidently something radically wrong in the system, and the advice of a medical man must be taken.

Sight, Dimness of. This may arise form effusion on the external part of the eye, or from disease of the retina that internal lining coating the eye, which receives the impression of external objects; but frequently a dimness of sight arises from a partial derangement of the retina, owing to a bad state of the digestive organs; for as the retina is an expansion of the optic nerve, and as the optic nerve has its source from that part of the brain where the nerves of the stomach arise, it is natural to think that when the stomach is deranged a partial effect must be evident on the eyes.

Treatment: When a person feels a dimness of sight, which upon examination he finds does not arise from external derangements of the coats of the eye, he should direct his attention to the treatment of the stomach; an emetic should be first taken, commencing on the day following with small doses of tincture of rhubarb, and continuing the dose daily; take also every morning a teaspoonful of the acidulated decoction of bark, and every seventh or eighth day a five-grain blue pill. The shower bath, good diet, change of air, and sea-bathing, are all excellent remedial measures. Bathe the eye with cold water, and use the following lotion: Sulphate of zinc, one grain; elder-flower water, one ounce; mix. When the eyes are watery and irritable, great benefit will be derived from laudanum, or sedative solution of

187

opium, painted several times over the lids and around the eye at night, and allowed to dry on, and washed off in the morning.

Sleep, Want of. The want of sleep, so distressing in itself, and so wearing to the system, may arise from a variety of causes; pain of the body and anxiety of mind are chief among these. But a person may be kept awake from some simple causes, as over-fatigue, want of out-door exercise, or overloaded stomach, cold feet, &c. Again sleeplessness may exist without any assignable reason.

Treatment: Adopt an easy, recumbent position, inclining the head towards the chest, shut the eyes and take several deep inspirations with the mouth closed.

Another: Tie a decanter-stopper with a bright, metallic top, a pencil-case, or any other bright object, on the forehead, in such a position that the eyes must be distorted or strained in order to see it. By resolutely gazing in this way for a short time, without winking, with the mind fully absorbed in the effort, the muscles of the eyes gradually relax, and the person falls asleep.

Another: Just before lying down, drink a tumbler-full of cold spring-water with a few grains of carbonate of potash in it.

Another: Having placed the body in a comfortable position, commence rolling the eyeballs backwards and forwards and upwards and downwards; continue doing this until sleep comes on, which will be generally in three or four minutes.

Another: Count slowly, with the eyes shut, from No. 1 to 100 or any other number necessary; in the midst of the counting, the person will in all probability fall asleep.

Another: Take a warm bath just before going to bed. A warm foot-bath will sometimes answer the purpose.

Another: Rub the body well with a rough towel or flesh-brush for a quarter of an hour, and go to bed immediately.

Another: Take a walk in the garden, or up and down the room, until the whole body feels in a warm glow, then go to bed immediately.

Another: Cut a Spanish onion into shreds, place it in a basin, and pour boiling vinegar over it; after letting it steep for a short time, eat it either alone or with the ordinary supper food. This mode of treating the onion deprives it in a great measure of its unpleasant taste and smell, while its sleep-inducing properties are but little impaired.

Another: Take twenty grains of carbonate of soda the last thing on going to bed.

Another: Take a teaspoon of paregoric elixir in a wine-glassful of water just before lying down. *Caution:* The habit of procuring sleep by indulgence in opium is exceedingly hurtful, for opium is injurious to the stomach, and loses its effect unless the dose be increased from night to night, which renders it still more injurious.

Sore Throat. This disease is most prevalent during the spring and autumn of the year, particularly among young people. It is usually the effect of cold caught after dancing, or by wet feet.

Treatment: When the throat is threatened, gargle it with diluted spirit of hartshorn, not so strong as to burn the mouth; rub in also, under the jaw, below the chin, the volatile liniment. Take meanwhile a saline purgative. *Or:* On the first appearance of difficulty swallowing take of senna tea a cupful, and dissolve in it three drachms of Epsom salts. Bathe the legs and feet in warm water, and go to bed with three or four folds of flannel about the neck; take spirit of mindererus, one ounce; antimonial wine, thirty drops; water, three ounces; syrup of squills, one drachm; mix, and take a tablespoonful every hour until perspiration is freely induced.

Spasms. Persons subject to confined bowels, if they have eaten anything which disagrees with them, are liable to this complaint.

Treatment: Take two large teaspoonfuls of antimonial wine every quarter of an hour, till the stomach be thoroughly relieved. Two hours afterwards, take one drachm of sal-volatile, with one ounce of castor oil.

Stomach-Ache: A complaint which usually arises from taking unwholesome or indigestible food.

Treatment: Take of magnesia one drachm; of rhubarb, half a drachm; powdered ginger, ten grains; divide into three powders; take one of these instantly, mixed in a little water, until it is quite smooth.

Another: For babies: Mix twenty trains of carbonate of magnesia in one ounce of dill-water, to which add ten drops of sal-volatile, give a teaspoonful when the child appears to be in pain.

Another: For children: Give to the child from a half to a teaspoonful of antimonial wine in a half a wine-glassful of warm water, and repeated every quarter of on hour, until the stomach is thoroughly relieved by vomiting. When this has been effected, give a dose of simple aperient medicine at bedtime, succeeded by a senna draught containing tincture of ginger.

Sunburns. A discoloration of the skin caused by exposure to the sun.

Treatment: Sweet cream, one ounce; new milk, eight ounces; juice of lemon, one ounce; alum, one ounce; sugar, one drachm. Boil and skim, and when the liquid is cool apply as a lotion to the face. Or take: Borax, fifteen grains; lemon juice, one ounce; sugar candy, half a drachm; mix the powders with the juice, and let them stand in a bottle, shaking them occasionally until they are dissolved.

Swooning. Persons of weak nerves or delicate constitutions are liable to fits of swooning. The general causes are sudden transition from cold to heat, breathing air deprived of its elasticity, great fatigue, loss of blood, long fasting, fear, grief, and other violent passions or affections of the mind.

Treatment: When anyone falls into a swoon, remove him immediately to a cooler apartment, apply ligatures above his knees and elbows, and sprinkle his hands and face with vinegar or cold water. He should likewise be made to smell the vinegar, and should have a spoonful or two of water, if he can swallow, with about a third part of vinegar mixed with it, poured into his mouth. If these should not remove the complaint, bleeding must be resorted to. When a person swoons from being exposed to vitiated air, or that of a theater, ball-room, &c., he ought immediately to be carried into the open air; his temples should be rubbed with strong vinegar or brandy, and sal volatile held to his nostrils. He should be laid upon his back with his head low, and have a little wine or some other cordial poured into his mouth as soon as he is able to swallow it. If the person has been subject to a hysterical fit, burnt feathers should be applied to the nostrils. *Observe:* Persons who are subject to swooning in public assemblies should place themselves near a door or window.

Teeth, Decayed. As soon as pain is felt in a tooth, however sound and beautiful it may appear outwardly, it is a certain sign of decay approaching and unless preservative means are instantly employed, the tooth will be lost.

Treatment: Bathe the feet in warm water, by means of which not only the tooth affected, but the rest will be preserved. The bathing must be continued until the pain is gone.

Observe: When the operation of stuffing the tooth is to be employed, it should be done when tooth-ache does not exist, otherwise it will give great uneasiness.

Caution: To prevent decay of the teeth, or to subdue it, avoid sweets, acids, hot or cold drinks, ices, &c. Do not pick the teeth with a pin nor suffer food to lodge in or between them. To prevent the latter, the mouth should be rinsed with warm water after every meal.

Tongue, Sore. The tongue is liable to become sore or ulcerated, most commonly, along the edges, and there are frequently seen small pimples and cracks.

Treatment: Take mild and cooling aperients, particularly calcined magnesia, either alone or in a Seidlitz powder. Let the drink be chiefly of soda water, and the diet be light and cooling. Touch the sores with burnt alum, and wash the mouth frequently with borax and honey dissolved in water, or a solution of chlorinated soda and water, so weak as not to produce much smarting.

Toothache. This well-known and very distressing pain may proceed from a variety of causes from sitting in draughts, inattention to the covering of the feet or the head, food or drink either too hot or too cold, and lastly from the presence of decay in the tooth itself. For a complaint so common there are, of course, innumerable remedies, and from these we select such as we believe to be the most efficacious.

Treatment: Apply stick-caustic to the part whence the pain proceeds.

Another: Take a tincture of opium, and rectified spirit of wine, of each three ounces; camphor, six drachms; opium powdered, one and a half drachms; pellitory of Spain, half ounce; macerate for eight days. Dip a small piece of lint into this mixture and place it in the cavity of the tooth.

Another: Apply oil of cloves on cotton wool.

Another: Moisten a piece of lint with a strong spirituous solution of creosote and closely ram it into the cavity of the tooth.

Another: Alum, in powder, two drachms; spirit of nitre, seven drachms; mix and apply to the tooth.

Observe: If neither of the above remedies avail, the tooth must be extracted; if suffered to remain, the teeth on either side will become affected.

Preventive: Those who are subject to toothache ought to be particular in keeping the teeth clean by the frequent use of a suft brush and water. The tooth powders most suitable are flowers of sulphur and charcoal powder; the former may be used every day, the latter twice a week. The best common charcoal powder should be employed, not the prepared charcoal, which is too often a compound of hurtful ingredients. When the gums are loose or spongy, the teeth should be cleaned three or four times a week with a powder, composed of equal parts of Peruvian bark, powder of catechu, and Armenian bole.

Varicose Veins. A varicose condition of the veins chiefly affects the legs, ankles, &c. The complaint consists essentially in the veins becoming elongated, in such a manner that they assume a knotted appearance, while they are at the same time enlarged. The most frequent causes of varicose veins are those which impede the upward flow of blood through the large veins of the abdomen; habitual costiveness, the wearing of a truss, or the tying of garters too tightly, will induce this disease; and it especially attacks women while bearing children.

Treatment: When the veins or the adjacent parts become inflamed and painful, leeches should be employed, and vinegar and water, Goulard water, or other cold lotion, constantly applied to the parts, or if cold applications do no good, the parts should be bathed with a warm decoction of poppy-heads, or warm water with laudanum. The bowels should be freely opened, by means of calomel and jalap, followed by Seidlitz powders, or any other cooling saline purgative. Low diet, quietude, and the recumbent position, are all essential to faster recovery. But, perhaps the best means of cure is the wearing of an elastic stocking, which supports the veins, and tends to remove the sense of weight and uneasiness which characterizes this complaint. Some persons cannot, however, wear an elastic stocking of any kind; for such cases, an elastic tape fixed to the foot by a stirrup and wound spirally round the limb, may be successfully employed. Spaces of about three inches being left between the spirals, each time the band crosses the vein it acts like a valve.

Voice, Loss of. Public speakers, singers, actors, &c., are subject to loss of voice, amounting in some instances, to extinction.

Treatment: Some camphor cigarettes made as follows: Select a sound and regular stalk of wheat straw; cut it evenly about an inch below and two or three inches above the knot; perforate the knot upwards with a stocking needle, and push down upon it through the larger end of the stalk, with a knitting needle, a small square of tissue paper. This paper covering the upper surface of the perforated knot forms a kind of medium between it and the air. The long end of the straw is then filled with some small pieces of camphor, loosely packed, and kept in place with a little plug of tissue paper. Close the lips firmly round the cigarettes, and draw as you would in smoking a pipe or cigar, but of course without the application of fire. The camphor thus inhaled finds its way direct to the respiratory organs, and affords considerable and speedy relief. A properly made cigarette will last a week; the camphor is to be renewed every night. The cigarette must be held between the lips alone, not by the teeth.

Another: Where the loss of voice results from the abuse of mercurial preparations, take of sarsaparill root a handful; water, one quart; boil for twenty minutes, and after taking the decoction off the fire, add fifteen grains of iodide of potassium. Dose, a wineglassful twice a day. Also, gargle the throat occasionally with salt water.

Vomiting. This may arise from various causes, as excess in eating and drinking, foulness of the stomach, the acrimony of aliments, sudden stoppage of wounds, weakness of the stomach, &c.

Treatment: When vomiting proceeds from foul stomach or indigestion, it is not to be considered as a disease, but as the cure of a disease. It ought, therefore, to be promoted by drinking lukewarm water or thin gruel. If this does not put a stop to the vomiting, a dose of ipecacuhana may be taken, and worked off with weak camomile tea.

Another: If vomiting proceed from the stomach, bitters will be of service. Peruvian bark infused in wine or brandy, with as much rhubarb as will open the body gently, is an excellent remedy in this case. The diluted acid of vitriol is also a good medicine, and may be taken in the dose of fifteen or twenty drops twice or thrice a day in a glass of wine or water. It has been said that habitual vomitings are alleviated by making oysters a part of the diet.

*Another:*When vomiting proceeds from violent passions or affections of the mind, all evacuants must be carefully avoided. The patient in this case ought to be kept perfectly easy and quiet, to have the mind soothed, and to take some gentle cordial, as negus or a little brandy and water, to which a few drops of laudanum may be occasionally added.

Another: When vomiting proceeds from spasmodic affections of the stomach, the application of a warm plaster to the pit of the stomach will afford relief. Any aromatic medicines may likewise be taken inwardly, as cinnamon or mint tea, wine with spices boiled in it, &c. The region of the stomach may be rubbed with ether, or if that cannot be had, with strong brandy or other spirit. The belly should be fomented with warm water, or the patient immersed up to the breast in a warm bath.

Observe: Saline draughts, taken in the act of effervescence, are of singular use in stopping a vomit, from whatever cause it may proceed. These draughts may be prepared by dissolving one drachm of the salt of tartar in one and a half ounces of fresh lemon juice, and adding to it one ounce of peppermint water, the same quantity of cinnamon water, and a little white sugar. This draught must be swallowed before the effervescence is quite over, and may be repeated every two hours or oftener, if the vomiting is violent. As the least motion will bring on vomiting again, even after it has stopped, the patient ought to avoid all manner of action.

Wasting. The rapid or gradual reduction of the size of the whole body or of parts thereof, frequently comes on without any evident cause. It is seldom accompanied by pain, difficulty of breathing, cough, or fever, but is usually attended with loss of appetite and impaired digestion, depression of spirits, and general languor.

Treatment: This disease is very difficult to cure, and for its treatment we must endeavour to find out the cause, and, if possible, remove it. If occasioned by worms, these must be destroyed by appropriate medicines; if by excess of any kind, this must be wholly discontinued; if from a scrofulous disposition, tonic medicines must be resorted to; and in like manner the treatment will be the same with that of every other disease which it may either accompany or of which it may the effect. The diet should be nutritious, generous, and such as is easy of digestion: milk, calves-feet jelly, together with a moderate proportion of beer and wine, and when the stomach is very feeble, spirits; regular walking exercise should be taken in the open air. The surface of the body should be well rubbed, and change of scene and sea-bathing may be resorted to. Of medicines, cod-liver oil is likely to prove the most effectual.

Observe: It often occurs, more particularly in children, that wasting takes place without derangement of any other process than that of nutrition. In these cases a teaspponful of cod-liver oil two or three time a day may often be followed by very decided and permanent benefit.

Watery Eye. If we look closely at the inner corner of the eyelids, we may perceive a little point at each, which is the opening of a duct that runs into the nose. These openings convey the tears from the eye, every time the eye is shut in winking, the fluid is forced into those pipes. Now, when either or both become so thickened as to be stopped up, the tears of necessity fall over the cheek, and this is called watery eye.

Treatment: As the cause of this disease is most commonly inflammation, it may be relieved in its early stages by a plan directed towards the lessening of that inflammation, and the best is as follows: Free the bowels well with salts, repeat this in three days afterwards, and apply the following eye-water: Take of common water two ounces, sulphate of zinc, four grains; laudanum, half a drachm; mix, and apply frequently. Cold must be strictly avoided.

Observe: If the complaint be not removed by the adoption of this treatment, surgical assistance must be obtained immediately for if the disease be allowed to proceed unchecked, the consequence will be a far more serious and troublesome affection.

Worms. The worms which infest the human body are of three kinds: the thread or maw-worm, half an inch long, terminating at its tail in a fine point; the lumbricord worm, or long round worm, when full grown, a foot in length, with triangular mouth; and the tape worm, body flat and joined, or body round, jointed, having a mouth at each joint. Although adults are subject to this complaint, it is most common with children. The signs are foetid breath, grinding of the teeth during sleep, picking at the nose, paleness of the face, acid eructations, swelling of a portion of the belly, which is there hard and tender, gripings, variable appetite, great irritability and itching of the lower parts of the body; short, dry cough; emaciation, slow fever, increasing toward night, irregular pulse and liability to convulsions.

Treatment: A dose of castor oil, exercise in the open air, wholesome diet and a strict prohibition of uncooked fruit, and raw and green vegetables; salt to be taken with all food eaten.

Or take: Filings of tin, cassia confection, of each half an ounce; syrup sufficient; mix. Take of the electuary a piece the size of a nutmeg twice a day; after this has been continued for two or three days, take of sub-muriate of mercury, three grains, powdered rhubarb, ten grains; mix, and take on the fourth morning after the receding.

Observe: The reason why children are more infested with worms than adults are, arises in a great measure from an indulgence in sweetmeats, sugar, &c., and from the partial or total neglect of salt. This matter should be scrupulously attended to, at the same time endeavoring to invigorate the system generally be wholesome and nutritious food. These measures are of themselves frequently sufficient to procure for a child an immunity from this distressing and debilitating complaint.

Ulcers. These generally proceed from some external injury, such as a wound or a bruise; or they arise in consequence of inflammation or some other disease. There are several sorts, as healthy, irritable, indolent inflamed, sloughing or gangrenous and sinous. They may be caused by wounds, injuries, bruises, inflammations, abscesses, or the suppression of some accustomed evacuation. Symptoms: A running sore, with acrid humours; hardness of the edges round the sore, and difficulty of healing.

Treatment: In the healthy, which secrete good matter, and look to be healing, though but slowly, poultice with white bread or linseed poultice for a day or two, then dress with the following: Olive oil, 16 ounces; yellow wax, 1 pound; yellow resin, 1 pound; Burgundy pitch, 1 pound; Venice turpentine, 3 ounces; melt the wax, resin and pitch together with the oil, over a slow fire. When mixed, take off the fire, and put in the turpentine; stir well and strain whilst hot through a coarse cloth.

In the irritable, which are very sore and spread, use the same fomentation as prescribed for rupture; take a cooling purgative, and use the following wash: Nitric or muriatic acid, fifty drops; water, one quart. Mix, and wash the sore with this two or three times a day, and poultice a day or two with linseed whilst using it. Then dress with the following salve: Venice turpentine, 1 ounce; frankincense, 1 ounce; beeswax, 1 ounce; linseed oil, 1 ounce; black rosin, 1 ounce; black pitch, 2 ounces. Melt together; when cold enough, add fresh butter (without salt) or lard, sufficient to make it soft enough to dress with; apply twice a day. When it begins to look healthy, dress with the yellow-wax ointment, as before recommended.

The indolent ulcers are often on the legs and require a similar treatment as the above. Persons suffering from bad and ulcerated legs, will find advantage in wearing elastic stockings.

Sudden Accidents and Injuries. These generally take place in travelling. The first thing is to remove any pressure on the body, and allow the air to come freely to the injured portion. If violent bleeding be perceived from any part, endeavor to arrest it, by placing on it a pad of folded linen and a bandage.

Fig. 54>>

Should it be a limb, and the blood be of a bright scarlet, tie a bandage tightly above the part; the tightness may be increased by inserting a piece of stick, and twisting it round, as in Fig. 55>>. Should no medical man be obtainable, the bleeding must be stopped by using a little hook called a tenaculum, the nearest approach to which is a shoemaker's sewing awl. This is put into the wound, and the vessel from which the blood flows hooked and drawn forward; a piece of silk is then tied round the vessel and if the blood ceases to flow, the wound is drawn together, and bound over with plaster. If blood is still ejected from the wound, there must be other arteries injured, which must be treated in the same manner before the wound be closed. Often pressure, long continued with the finger, will stop the bleeding, as in Fig. 56>>. If no wound be perceptible, and the lips and face pale, the hands and feet cold, lay the person out flat, apply warmth to the body, and administer a little brandy and water every few minutes, and afterwards beef-tea, for if the person has only fainted he will speedily recover; but if the injury be greater, the remedies must be persevered in for hours, and every attention rendered. Should the effects proceed from a blow, that is, the person be stunned, then raise the head, apply warmth to the feet, and some pungent smelling-salts to the nose. If the flesh be cut, bathe with a sponge and cold water until all the dirt be cleared away and the bleeding stop; then bring the edges of the wound carefully together, and keep them so by strips of sticking-plaster, Fig. 57>>. On the extremities, a piece of linen may be laid over the wound, and then bandaged. But should the wound be extensive, take a needle threaded with silk, dip it in oil, and enter the skin about one-eight of an inch deep; tie each stitch with a knot, Fig. 58>>, and about thirty hours afterward cut the silk, and draw out the thread. If the

198

part have a throbbing sensation, bathe it with cold water. In cases where the flesh is torn, bring the parts gently together, and lightly strap them with sticking-plaster. If a part be bruised, let it remain as much at rest as possible; but, if severe, get the person to bed, and apply a cloth dipped in cold water every few minutes. Should the part bleed, the vessel can be tied as before directed. Many persons feel themselves shaken without any positive injury; but we would advise, in this case, that at least an hour's rest be taken on a couch or bed.

Cuts. For small and simple cuts, use the following.

Treatment: Tie it up at once with a piece of linen rag; this is usually sufficient to stay the bleeding. The small quantity of blood which may exude quickly dries up the wound, and forms a sort of glue which effectually excludes the air. As no better dressing can be used, it may be left on till the cut is well. If the bleeding should be excessive, it should be checked by the use of cold water or astringents, such as turpentine or Friar's balsam, and the edges of the cut surface brought firmly into contact by strips of sticking-plaster, and, if necessary, bandaged.

Cuts from the Flesh. If a piece of flesh be cut out, wash it and the part from which it was cut, without a moments's loss of time, replace it exactly in its proper place, and keep it there with a piece of sticking-plaster. If the piece cannot be replaced, bathe the part with cold water until the bleeding stops, and place over it a piece of soft linen, as directed in Fig. 54>>.

Stabs. The danger of such accidents is, that there may be some important deeply-seated part injured. They are treated as common wounds: the bleeding stopped by cold water and a sponge, then the edges brought together with strapping, and bound up. If inflammation set in, foment with cold water for a day or two, then with warm water, and apply poultices. At times, when apparently healing, there will be a painful sensation, and matter formed below will force its way out; this may happen more than once. The patient should be kept quiet in bed for several days.

Glossary

animalcule = microscopic animal, invisible to the naked eye
bole = reddish brown color, often derived from clay
buchu = *Virginus barosma* native shrub of Cape Colony
cantharides = *Lytta vesicatoria,* Spanish Fly, blister beetle
cascarilla = *Croton eleuteria,* tree yielding fragrant resin
catechu = gum, resin of *Acacia catechu*
cinchona = quinine, from trees or shrubs of genus *Cinchona*
colocynth = bitter aromatic, fruit of *Citrullus colocynthis*
copaiba, balsam = resin of S. Amer. plant *Copaifera*
costiveness = constipation
croton oil = violent cathartic from seeds of *Croton tiglium*
cubebs = unripe dried berries of *Piper cubeba*
cupping = drawing blood with heated cupping glasses
demulcent = soothing medication
diluents = diluting substances
Dover's powder = mix of opium & ipecacuanha, induces sweating
drachm (dram, dr.) = 1/8 oz. apothecary weight, 1/16 oz. av.
electuary = drugs made into paste to be taken by mouth
embrocation = liniment or lotion for rubbing
excoriation = stripping off or removing skin
fomentation = sponging with warm or hot liquid
Goulard water = solution of sub-acetate, early disinfectant
grain (grs) = one grain = 65 milligrams
guaiacum = *Guaiacum officinale*, spice and medicine
henbane = *Hyoscyamus niger*, deadly nightshade
Hoxham's Tincture = see Cinchona, above
jalap = from the root of *Ipomoea jalapa*
lobule = a small lobe
manna = weeping sap of *Fraximus ornus*, source of manitol
mendererus or mindererus = acetate of ammonia
nitre = potassium nitrate, saltpeter
opodeldoc = liniment made of soap with spices or opium
pellitory = oil of *Anacyclus pyrethrum*
Peruvian bark = bark of *Cinchona spp*, contain quinine
rhubarb = root is powerful laxative

Rochelle Salt = potassium sodium tartrate
sal volatile = aromatic alcoholic solution of ammonium carbonate
scammony = *Convolvulus scammonia*, here used as cathartic
scruple = 20 grains, an apothecary weight
Seidlitz Powder = mild laxative
squills = *Urginea scilla*, sea onion
stramonium = dried leaves of datura or jimson weed; poisonous
throw up = inject with syringe for enema, douche, etc.
tolu = expectorant, resin of *Myroxylon balsamum*
wormwood = *Artemisia absinthium*; essentially poisonous.

NAMES

Burns, Robert, poet, 1759-1796, Scottish poet
Byron, George Gordon, Lord, 1788-1824, English poet
Darwin, Erasmus (the Elder), 1731-1802, English naturalist and
        poet, grandfather of Charles Darwin
Granville, George, Earl of, 1815-1891, English industrialist
Pancoast, Dr. Joseph, 1805-1882, Prof. of surgery and anatomy,
        Jefferson Medical College
Stael, Mme. de, 1766-1817, French writer
Tennison, Alfred Lord, 1809-1892, English Poet Laureate

Artists' credits for drawings:
Agassiz, Bischoff, Rathke, and Tander

Fig. 1. Section of
Pistil with pollen
grains sending
down tubes.

Fig. 5. Renal Gland.
Malpigian bodies
from kidneys of owl.
Convoluting tubes.

Fig. 6. Back View of Body.
1, Lungs. 2, Stomach.
3, Kidneys. 4, Ureters

Fig. 7. Course of Circulation.
a, encloses 4 heart chambers.
b, veins bring dark blood to
c, right auricle, d, right ventricle

Fig. 9. Human
Spermatozoa, 900 to
1000 times magnified.
a, flat surface; b, in
profile; c, granules or
cells in which other
zoosperms are preparing.

Fig. 10. Evolution of Zoosperm,
1000 times magnified.
a, large corpuscle;
b, globule with 3 enclosed bodies;
c, bundle of animalcules as grouped
    in testicle.

Fig. 11. Cyst of Evolution.
Seminal cyst or cell enclosing,
a, 5 smaller cells, each with nucleus;
b, 2 germinal granules, magnified

Fig. 12. An Ovum.
a, germinal spot;
b, germinal vesicle;
c, yolk; d, zona pellucida
e, discus poligonus;
f, adhering granules or cells.

Fig. 13. Mammal Ovum
Ovum of a Bitch, 23 days since last access to a male. The chorion, c, has already shot forth little villi, which are wanting at each end b of the ovum and also over the place where the embryo is situated.

Fig. 14, Ova in the Ovary of a Bird.
Two eggs of a bird as found in the ovary, barely perceptible to the human eye.
a, stroma, thick fibres; c, Chorion, external membrane of ovum; b, yolk; d, germinal vesicle; e, germinal spot, which is the real germ from which the embryo evolves.

Fig. 15. Ovary and Oviduct from a laying Hen.
a, immature ovarian eggs;
b, mature ovarian egg;
c, opening of the duct which receives egg.

Fig. 16. Ovaries, etc., of the Bee.
o, o, ovaries; t, t, t, oviducts;
e, e, e, eggs in oviducts;
g, receptaculum seminis;
n, j, sting; s, poison bag.

Fig. 17. Ideal Section of a Hen's Egg. The egg of the fowl is the type of all ova and from its large size easy to study.

A, blunt pole; B, sharp pole; a, a, shell; b, space filled with air to supply oxygen; c, membrane of shell, which at d, d, splits into two layers; e, e, limits of second, thicker albumen; f, limit of thickest albumen; g,g, chalaze or twisted fibres from yolk, which holds it in place. h, yolk; i, central cavity in the yolk from which a duct, k, leads to the cicatricula, or tread. l, cumulus proligerous, or germinal cumulus; m, germ or blastos. The egg is so formed that the yolk floats high in the white, and the germ is always uppermost.

Fig. 18. Egg 36 hours after Incubation.

Fig. 19. Egg opened 3 days after incubation.

Fig. 20. Unimpregnated Egg after disappearance of the germinal disk and adherent granules.

Fig. 21. Human Egg during segmentation into two parts.

Fig. 22. The Human Egg undergoing segmentation into four parts.

Fig. 23. Further subdivisions of the human egg during segmentation, called the mulberry stage.

Fig. 25. Human Ovum.
Size of Nature.

Fig. 26. Human Ovum
Laid Open.

Fig. 27. Corpuslets of Blood.
Seen flat and on edge.

Fig. 29. Brain and Nerve.
Primitive fibres and ganglionic globules
after Purkinje. b. from dark portion of
crus cerebri.

Fig. 30. Placenta and Umbilical Cord,
Blood vessels seen from foetal side.

Fig. 31. Embryo of a Dog.
Highly magnified from the
Abdominal aspect.

Fig. 32. Embryo Chicken.
From middle of the third day, four
lines long. b, c, d, are hemispheres of
the brain; e the cerebellum, i ventricle
of the heart. This resembles the human
embryo at same stage of development
but later period.

Fig. 33. Embryo of Fowl at
Eight days.

Fig 34. Circulation of a Fish
before hatching.

Fig. 35. Circulation of Chicken
at early state of growth in egg.

Fig. 36. Circulation of Embryo
of Guinea Pig on 18th day of
Gestation.

Fig. 37. Circulation of a Snapping
Turtle at early stage of growth in
the egg.

Fig. 38. Circulation of a Snake
at an early stage of growth in
the egg.

Fig. 39. Microscopic elements of nervous structure. 1, three loops are simple, one convoluted. 3. White nerve fiber enlarged to show its structure.

Fig. 40. Origin of the Milk Ducts.

Fig. 41. Ultimate Follicles of the Mammary Glands. a, secreting cells, b, the Nuclei.

Fig. 43.   Fig. 44.

Fig. 45.   Fig. 46.

Fig. 47.   Fig. 48.

Fig. 49.   Fig. 50.

Fig. 51   Fig. 52.

Figures 43 to 52. Progressing malformation of Urethra, obstructed passages, false passages made by a bougie, Extensive ulceration and a fistulous opening through which the urine flowed.

Fig. 54. Arrest violent bleeding with a pad and a folded linen bandage.

Fig. 55. If a limb is cut off, increase tightness of bandage by inserting a stick and twisting till bleeding ceases.

Fig. 56. Often pressure long continued as shown here will stop bleeding.

Fig. 57. If flesh be cut, bring the edges together and tape.

Fig. 58. For extensive wounds, thread a needle with silk, dip in oil, enter skin 1/8 inch deep, tie each stitch with a knot. Cut silk and remove thread thirty hours later.